CONTENTS

SERIES EDITOR'S INTRODUCTION

One measure of methodological progress is the ability to handle complication. The world observed appears incredibly complex, a swirl of noisy variables. To make sense of it, the analyst may first move to multiple regression (ordinary least squares—OLS), with its capacity for sorting independent effects under conditions of statistical control. The textbook three-variable model follows:

$$Y = a + bX + cZ + e \qquad (1)$$

where

Y = dependent variable
X and Z = independent variables
a = intercept
b and c = slopes
e = error

Equation (1) follows the usual assumption, that the impact of X on Y is independent of the particular value of Z. But is the world more complicated than that? Specifically, does the impact of X depend on the value Z holds? If "yes," then there is an interaction effect, which implies that a product term should be included, such as

$$Y = a + bX + cZ + d(X \times Z) + e. \qquad (2)$$

Procedures for incorporating interaction effects, in the context of traditional multiple regression analysis, are fully spelled out in the earlier, companion series volume (Jaccard, Turrisi, and Wan, No. 72). The work at hand advances the evaluation of interactions several additional steps, through use of structural equation modeling (SEM), with latent variables and LISREL estimation. More important, the real complications of multiple indicators and measurement error, two conditions that OLS stumbles over, are made manageable. (For background on SEM, LISREL, and latent variables, see the following works in the series: Long, Nos. 34, 35; Hagenaars, No. 94).

Drs. Jaccard and Wan give a careful exposition of LISREL computer programming and its application to SEM. A model can be input with eight different matrices. The explication is doubly useful, because of the continuing evolution of LISREL, now in its eighth version. Along the way, key points are emphasized, such as the selection of the reference variable in order to define the metric of the latent variable. Also, a valuable

v

comparative discussion of goodness-of-fit measures for LISREL models is offered, including the widely used chi-square test. Regarding that test, they make its "reverse" logic clear—the model receives support when the chi-square falls short of significance. The specific chi-square test for an interaction is "two-step." In the first step, the fit is not constrained (e.g., slopes are permitted to be different from one group to the next). In the second step, the fit is constrained (e.g., slopes are not permitted to be different from one group to the next). The results are then compared, to see if the unconstrained model (which allows interaction) fits better. If an interaction effect is present, its size (IES) can be measured as a reduction in the Step 2 chi-square.

Like multiple regression, product terms can be used with LISREL, given that all the variables are continuous. Where appropriate, the authors contrast the SEM (with multiple indicators and measurement error) approach to an OLS approach. They observe that there are trade-offs between the two approaches, concluding that under conditions of high measurement reliability, small sample size, and lack of multivariate normality, OLS may perform better. Obviously, these conditions are not always met, in which case SEM merits serious exploration when the analyst wishes sophisticated, more realistic, models of interaction effects.

Michael S. Lewis-Beck
Series Editor

PREFACE

This monograph is a companion to our earlier book *Interaction Effects in Multiple Regression* (Sage QASS No. 72, by Jaccard, Turrisi, and Wan). In this monograph, we guide the reader through the use of the computer program LISREL and how it can be applied to multiple-indicator analyses of interactions in regression frameworks. We assume that the reader is familiar with the material in our previous monograph, but we assume no prior knowledge of LISREL or structural equation models. Readers with limited background in structural equation modeling can consult other texts to familiarize themselves with the complex issues involved in such model testing (e.g., Bollen, 1989; Bollen & Long, 1993; Loehlin, 1987).

Our approach is pedagogically oriented and will disappoint more technically oriented readers. Our goal is to introduce the general analytic strategy to the reader so that he or she can gain a general overview of the analytic methods. This is an introductory treatment aimed at the applied researcher with a reasonable background in traditional multiple regression. It is not intended to be a text on structural equation modeling. Because of page restrictions, we were unable to discuss many topics that more experienced analysts probably would have liked us to consider. To counteract this, we have directed the reader to additional resource materials that we have found to be useful. Wherever possible, we have provided practical recommendations for analysts based on the current literature. At times, this was difficult because of a paucity of research on the issue in question. Rather then leave the analyst hanging, we decided to give our "best guess" in terms of practical advice, recognizing full well that future research may alter our recommendations and that some analysts may disagree with our recommendations.

Although there are other statistical packages that focus on the analysis of structural equations, we chose the LISREL program because of its widespread use and the fact that the most recent version (LISREL 8.12) permits nonlinear constraints among parameters. Such constraints are central to many forms of interaction analysis. EQS, the main competitor of LISREL, currently does not have this capability. CALIS (within SAS) and programs such as COSAN have such capabilities, but, in our opinion, they are less user friendly than LISREL.

In addition, CALIS and COSAN do not permit multiple group analyses, a technique that we rely on. We use standard LISREL programming instead of the easier SIMPLIS language within LISREL because SIMPLIS currently does not permit nonlinear constraints. The programming method we teach is inefficient and at times cumbersome, but we have found it to be pedagogically sound and easy for readers to understand. As the reader gains more experience with LISREL, programming shortcuts can be adopted.

vii

As in our previous monograph, the material in the present volume is limited to the analysis of interaction effects for which the primary predictor variable as well as the criterion variable are continuous in nature (although the moderator variable may be either qualitative or quantitative). The case in which all predictors are qualitative (and the dependent variable is continuous) reduces to either traditional analysis of variance or multivariate analysis of variance. For discussions of the use of structural equation modeling in these cases, see Kenny (1979), Kuhnel (1988), Bray and Maxwell (1985), and Cole, Maxwell, Arvey, and Salas (1993).

Several colleagues provided useful feedback on previous drafts of this manuscript. We would like to thank David Brinberg, Carol Carlson, and John Lynch for their helpful comments. The two anonymous reviewers provided excellent suggestions for improving the manuscript. The series editor, Michael Lewis-Beck, was especially supportive and constructive during the development of both this monograph and the previous one. We are much indebted to him.

LISREL APPROACHES TO INTERACTION EFFECTS IN MULTIPLE REGRESSION

JAMES JACCARD
CHOI K. WAN
University at Albany, State University of New York

1. INTRODUCTION

The analysis of interaction effects between continuous variables in multiple regression has been receiving increased attention (e.g., Aiken & West, 1991; Jaccard, Turrisi, & Wan, 1990). Recent articles lament problems inherent in the analysis of interactions in field research and observational studies (e.g., McClelland & Judd, 1993). These include problems resulting from measurement error and the low statistical power that can result from such error. This monograph presents an approach for confronting these problems, namely the use of multiple indicators and structural equation modeling (SEM).

Consider the following research example. An investigator believes that peer pressure influences adolescent drug use, such that the stronger the pressure from peers to use drugs, the more likely it is that an adolescent will use drugs. The researcher also hypothesizes, however, that the impact of peer pressure on drug use may be moderated by the relationship that the adolescent has with his or her parents. When the parent-teen relationship is poor, peer pressure will have a large impact on drug use; however, when the parent-teen relationship is good, the impact of peer pressure will be diminished.

One strategy for testing this hypothesis is to use multiple regression analysis. Suppose that data are collected from a group of 800 adolescents, containing quantitative measures of the three variables. Drug use (Y) is measured on a 7-point scale, with higher scores indicating greater drug use. Peer pressure (X) is measured on a 10-point scale, with higher scores implying greater pressure to use drugs. The quality of the parent-teen relationship (Z) is measured on a 7-point scale, with higher scores indicating a better relationship. In this analysis, Y is the criterion or dependent variable, X is the predictor or independent variable, and Z is the moderator variable that influences or "moderates" the impact of X on Y. The regression model traditionally used to test for (bilinear) interaction uses a product term such that

$$Y = \alpha + \beta_1 X + \beta_2 Z + \beta_3 XZ + \varepsilon \qquad (1.1)$$

If the test of β_3 is statistically significant, then the null hypothesis of no interaction effect is rejected, given that the residual term meets the traditional assumptions of

1

multiple regression. The estimated value of β_3 provides information about the nature of the interaction. Specifically, it indicates how much the slope of Y on X is predicted to change given a one unit change in the moderator variable, Z. Suppose, for example, that the sample estimate of β_3 was -3.5. This means that for every one unit that the quality of the parent-teen relationship increases, the impact of peer pressure on drug use (i.e., the slope of drug use on peer pressure) is predicted to decrease by 3.5 units.[1]

Although such analyses are straightforward, they are fraught with a fundamental problem in social science data, namely the problem of measurement error. Social science data frequently are measured with error; that is, measures are *fallible*. This error can produce bias in the estimates of β_3 and can undermine significance tests. Sometimes the bias is substantial. For example, if the correlation between X and Z is 0 and the measures of X and Z each have a reliability of 0.70, then the reliability of the product term, XZ, will be the product of the reliabilities of X and Z, or 0.49. The proportion of variance in the dependent variable that is explained by an interaction effect measured with this amount of error would be less than half the magnitude of the true interaction effect size! Such low levels of reliability reduce statistical power and negatively bias the estimate of β_3. It thus becomes important to use statistical methods that can accommodate measurement error. Traditional regression analysis does not do so.

This monograph is an introduction to analytic methods that deal with the problem of measurement error in the analysis of interactions. We consider a wide range of applications, including qualitative moderator variables, longitudinal designs, and product term analysis. In this chapter, we first describe different types of measurement error. We then formulate latent variable representations of measurement error, which serve as the foundation for analyses described in later chapters. Finally, we provide a brief introduction to the computer program LISREL, which is used to execute the analyses.

Types of Measurement Error

There are three types of measurement error that are relevant for our purposes. The first type focuses on the scale metric: We assume that our data are interval level when, in fact, they may only be ordinal level. The analytic strategies discussed in this monograph assume that measures of continuous variables are interval level. In practice, this may not be true, thereby introducing measurement error. Many of the measures used in the social sciences are ordinal in character. These data nevertheless can be analyzed effectively using statistics that assume interval level measures if departures from intervalness are not extreme. This latter statement requires elaboration.

Some researchers erroneously refer to scales as being interval or ordinal in character. For example, it is frequently stated that Likert-type scales are ordinal. It is important to recognize that metric qualities are not inherent in scales but rather are inherent in data and, hence, are influenced by all the facets of data collection. The extent to which a set of measures has interval properties is dependent not only on the scale used to make observations but also on the particular set of individuals on which the observations are made, the time at which the data are collected, the setting in which the data are collected, and so on. Consider the following simplistic yet pedagogically useful example. The height of five individuals is measured on two different metrics, inches and a rank order of height:

Individual	Height in Inches	Rank Order
A	72	5
B	71	4
C	70	3
D	69	2
E	67	1

As is well known, the measures taken in inches have interval level properties. For example, a difference of 1 between any two scores corresponds to the same physical difference on the underlying dimension of height. The actual height difference between individuals A and B corresponds to the same true underlying height difference between individuals C and D, and the metric reflects this (i.e., $72 - 71 = 1$ and $70 - 69 = 1$). Similarly, the difference between D and E is $69 - 67 = 2$, and the difference between A and C is 2. These two differences also reflect the same amount on the underlying dimension of height. Note, however, that these properties do not hold for the rank order measures. The difference in scores between individuals A and B is 1 (i.e., $5 - 4$), and the difference in scores for individuals D and E is also 1 (i.e., $2 - 1$). These identical differences correspond to differing degrees of height disparities (i.e., the true difference between individuals D and E is larger than the true difference between individuals A and B, as is evident for the measure using inches). For these individuals, the rank order measures have ordinal properties but do not have interval properties.

Now consider five different individuals with the following scores:

Individual	Height in Inches	Rank Order
A	72	5
B	71	4
C	70	3
D	69	2
E	68	1

Note that for these five individuals, the rank order measures have interval level properties. The difference in scores between individuals A and B is 1, as is the difference between individuals D and E. These differences correspond to exactly the same distance on the underlying physical dimension. In this case, what we think of as traditionally being an ordinal "scale" actually yields measures with interval level properties. Suppose that individual E was not 68" tall but instead was 67.9" tall. In this case, the rank order measures are not strictly interval, but they are close and probably can be treated as if they are interval level.

This example illustrates that the crucial analytic issue is not whether a set of measures is interval or ordinal. Rather, the critical issue is the extent to which a set of measures *approximates* interval level characteristics. If the approximation is close, then the data often can be analyzed effectively using statistical methods that assume interval level properties. If the approximation is poor, an alternative analytic strategy is called for. Psychologists have developed methods for ascertaining the degree of approximation to intervalness (see, e.g., Anderson, 1981, 1982; Wegener, 1982). These methods are neither perfect nor universally applicable, but they can be used effectively in a wide variety of contexts. Numerous Monte Carlo studies have been undertaken to examine the effects of differing degrees of departure from intervalness on parametric statistics. For many statistical tests, rather severe departures do not seem to affect Type I and Type II errors dramatically. This complex literature defies simple characterization, however, and interested readers are referred to Bohrnstedt and Carter (1971), Busemeyer and Jones (1983), Townsend (1990), and Townsend and Ashby (1984). This monograph will not consider this particular form of measurement error and will assume that approximations to intervalness are sufficiently close that they do not undermine further analysis.

The two additional forms of measurement error are *random* measurement error and *systematic* measurement error. Random error traditionally is associated with the concept of reliability and reflects random influences that can bias observed scores upward or downward. For example, an individual's response to an opinion item on an attitude questionnaire might be influenced because he or she misreads the item (although at a future time, if the attitude scale is repeated, he or she may not misread the item again, giving rise to a different response). The reliability of a measure is the extent to which that measure is free of random error. A measure that has a reliability of 0.80 is such that 20% of its variance is random error and 80% of its variance is systematic.

Systematic measurement error is error that is nonrandom and reflects factors that systematically create variation in a measure but that have nothing to do with the underlying construct being measured. A common source of systematic measurement error is social desirability bias. For example, rather than measuring drug use exclusively, a measure might also reflect a person's willingness to admit to drug use. Both random and systematic measurement error can distort estimates of β_3 in Equation 1.1. The procedures discussed in this monograph can be used to help offset these distorting influences.

Latent Variable Representations of Measurement Error

We can formally represent measurement error for variables by using path diagrams, such as that presented in Figure 1.1. The measure of drug use, referred to as D1, is indicated by a square or rectangle. The true amount of drug use (which we can never know directly) is indicated by a circle and is referred to as a *latent variable*. Presumably, the true amount of drug use influences responses to the observed measure; hence, the straight causal arrow linking the two. In addition to the influence of the true construct, other factors can influence the observed measure. These influences are reflected in an error term called e. This term reflects all other variables (both random and systematic) that cause variation in the observed measure.

We can now recast Equation 1.1 into a path diagram that reflects the regression analysis for the underlying latent variables as well as a measurement model that reflects the presence of measurement error in each of the measures. This is presented in Figure 1.2. P1, Q1, and

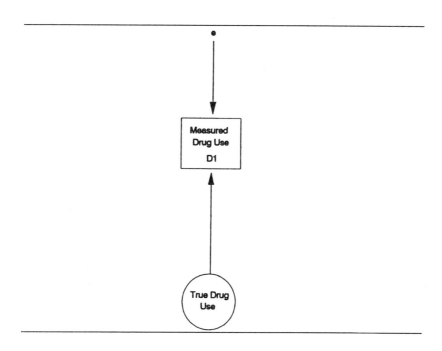

Figure 1.1. Latent Variable With Observed Variable and Measurement Error

D1 are the observed measures of the latent variables. The product term P1Q1 is the observed measure of the latent product term. Causal paths between the latent variables are denoted by the letter p, and these are interpreted as regression coefficients. In path diagrams, however, regression coefficients are called path coefficients. Thus, p_3 is directly analogous to β_3 (although it is represented here as a sample statistic, as noted by the absence of Greek notation). Path coefficients exist not only between latent predictor variables and latent criterion variables but also from latent variables to observed indicators (although these are not notated with p's in Figure 1.2). A path coefficient signifies a proposed causal link between two variables and is interpreted as the predicted amount of change in the criterion variable given a one unit change in the predictor variable (holding all other variables constant). In addition to the measurement errors (e), there is a residual term, E, that is associated with the latent drug use variable. This term represents all other factors that influence drug use other than the three predictors with arrows going to drug use. E is assumed to be uncorrelated with the three latent predictor variables, a standard assumption in regression analysis. Of primary theoretical interest is the value and significance test for p_3, because it represents an estimate of the interaction effect.

The above characterizations assume that we have one measure of each construct. Suppose that instead of a single measure of drug use, we have three measures of drug

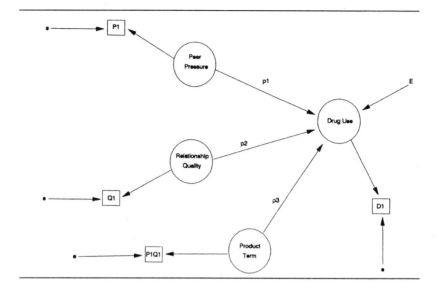

Figure 1.2. Path Model for Effects of Peer Pressure and Relationship Quality on Drug Use

use, each of which is construed as an interchangeable *indicator* of true drug use. Suppose further that we have three indicators of peer pressure and three indicators of the quality of the parent-teen relationship, yielding a total of nine measures. This implies a new path model, which is presented in Figure 1.3.

The three measures of drug use are D1, D2, and D3. Each is influenced by the latent variable representing true drug use as well as measurement error. The three indicators of peer pressure are P1, P2, and P3, and the indicators of parent-teen relationship quality are Q1, Q2, and Q3. Each measure is assumed to be fallible. The curved line linking the latent variables indicates that the variables are assumed to be correlated but that there is no formal causal relationship between them (we explain the other curved line for the drug use residuals in the next section). In the present example, the latent product term is assumed to be uncorrelated with the other latent predictor variables (a scenario that would hold if mean-centered scores are used and the nonproduct latent predictor variables are multivariately normally distributed). Sometimes the curved lines between latent predictors are omitted in order to reduce clutter, and the presence of latent X correlations is noted in a footnote at the bottom of the figure. The latent product term has nine indicators that are represented by all possible product terms among the three indicators of peer pressure and the three indicators of relationship quality.

The advantage of a multiple-indicator model like that depicted is that the multiple indicators can be used to estimate the effects of measurement error, and estimates of the regression coefficients between the true latent variables can be derived taking this measure-

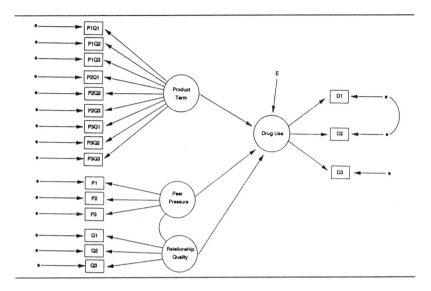

Figure 1.3. Multiple-Indicator Path Model for Effects of Peer Pressure and Relationship Quality on Drug Use

ment error into account. This is a distinct advantage relative to single-indicator models and suggests that when possible, high-quality multiple indicators should be sought.

Correlated Versus Uncorrelated Error

The model of drug use that we have described assumes that all the error terms are uncorrelated. Let us examine this assumption more closely for one of our constructs, drug use. The measures D1 and D2 are assumed to be influenced by a common latent variable (true drug use); hence, D1 and D2 should be correlated because they have a common cause. The error terms for D1 and D2 are assumed to be uncorrelated. Suppose, however, that there is systematic error in the data that is influencing both D1 and D2. Both D1 and D2 are self-reports of drug use and both might be influenced by social desirability tendencies. This means that part of the error of D1 consists of social desirability tendencies and part of the error of D2 also consists of social desirability tendencies. The presence of social desirability in both error terms suggests that the two errors are correlated. Using this logic, we now add a curved line between the two errors to reflect this common source (see Figure 1.3).

When formulating path models, it is necessary to think carefully about where correlated errors might be present. In short, the theorist must develop an error theory to complement the structural theory linking latent variables. This is particularly important for the analysis of product terms, because the errors of the product indicators will be correlated in complex ways (see Chapter 4).

Measurement Precision

Another important concept in structural equation analysis is that of measurement precision. Our primary focus in this monograph is on continuous latent variables. It is rare in practice, however, that the observed indicators of such latent variables are continuous. An observed measure usually consists instead of a finite set of ordered categories that (ideally) have interval level properties. For example, a measure of the underlying continuous variable "intelligence" might range from 0 to 25, with higher scores indicating more intelligence.

The precision of a measure refers to the number of discriminations that the measure makes. An intelligence test that yields scores ranging from 0 to 100 is a more "precise" measure than one that yields scores ranging from 0 to 25. Measurement precision can affect model analysis in structural equation modeling, with less precise measures introducing analytic complications. We will assume that all the examples in this monograph use sufficiently precise measures so as to permit traditional structural modeling.

Analyzing Multiple-Indicator Models: An Introduction to LISREL

The computer program that we will use to analyze multiple-indicator models is LISREL 8. Readers who are already familiar with LISREL can skip the following section and move directly to Chapter 2. We will develop the logic of LISREL programming using a regression example with multiple indicators but with no interaction effects. The introduction of product terms complicates the analysis, and it is better to introduce the procedures with a simpler example.

Consider an example in which an educator is testing a theory that a child's desire to achieve in school (Y) is influenced by his or her mother's achievement orientation (X) and his or her father's achievement orientation (Z). In traditional multiple regression, this can be expressed as a simple linear model:

$$Y = \alpha + \beta_1 X + \beta_2 Z + \varepsilon \qquad (1.2)$$

Suppose we have three indicators of each variable. Specifically, C1, C2, and C3 are indicators of child achievement orientation, and each is measured on a scale ranging from 1 to 10. M1, M2, and M3 are indicators of mother achievement orientation, and each is also measured on a scale ranging from 1 to 10. F1, F2, and F3 are indicators of father achievement orientation, and each is measured on a scale ranging from 1 to 10. Figure 1.4 presents the path diagram for the model. We assume uncorrelated errors between the residuals, although this need not always be the case. Our task is to convey to LISREL the form of the model so that parameter estimates can be derived and the model can be tested against the data.

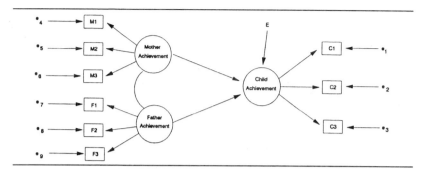

Figure 1.4. Multiple-Indicator Path Model for Effects of Mother Achievement Orientation and Father Achievement Orientation on Child Achievement Orientation

The first part of the LISREL program is straightforward and conveys basic information about the input data. Here are the first five lines:

```
ANALYSIS OF CHILD ACHIEVEMENT
DA NO=278 NI=9
LA
C1 C2 C3 M1 M2 M3 F1 F2 F3
CM FI = CHILD.DAT
```

Line 1 is a title line. Line 2 is a data line that must begin with the letters DA. It conveys basic data input information. NO is the sample size (number of observations, which in this case equals 278) and NI is the total number of variables (NI = 9). Line 3 indicates that labels will be provided for the variables and begins with the letters LA. The actual labels must appear on a separate line that follows the LA line. Line 4 provides the labels for the input variables, with a blank separating each label. The labels must be in the same order in which the data are input. There is a limit of eight characters per label. Line 5 tells LISREL to retrieve the file named CHILD.DAT and read in a covariance matrix (CM). The covariance matrix is in lower triangular form and is the covariance matrix between all the observed variables in the order that they are listed on line 4. The entries in the file CHILD.DAT are in free format form, meaning that numbers are separated by either a blank or a comma. In this example, the file CHILD.DAT would appear as follows:

```
17.3
16.3 17.5
16.4 16.4 17.3
 5.1  5.1  5.1  5.6
 5.0  5.0  5.0  4.7  5.8
```

```
5.7   5.6   5.6   4.9   5.1   6.2
5.4   5.5   5.7   0.3   0.2   0.2   5.9
5.6   5.8   5.9   0.5   0.3   0.6   4.9   5.9
5.4   5.5   5.7   0.4   0.2   0.3   4.7   4.7   5.6
```

The data can appear in any format (e.g., a single number per line), but it must be in the order implied by a lower triangle symmetric matrix (i.e., 17.3 must be first, then 16.3, then 17.5, and so on).

LISREL makes distinctions between latent X variables and latent Y variables. A latent Y variable is one that is influenced by at least one other latent variable. In our example, child achievement orientation is a latent Y variable because it is influenced by the latent mother achievement orientation and the latent father achievement orientation variables. A latent X variable is one that is not influenced by any latent variables. In our example, mother and father achievement orientations are latent X variables because neither is influenced by any other latent variable in the system. The latent Y variable has three indicators (C1, C2, C3), and these are called observed Y variables. The latent X variables also have indicators (M1, M2, M3, F1, F2, F3), and these are called observed X variables. For LISREL to work properly, the observed Y variables must appear first in the covariance matrix, followed by the observed X variables. If the variables are in a different order when they are read in with the first five lines of the program, they can be rearranged using a Select command. It is optional and would appear as follows:

```
SE
C1 C2 C3 M1 M2 M3 F1 F2 F3
```

The first line begins with SE and indicates that the select feature is to be activated. The second line specifies the order the rearranged variables should have, using the labels from the LA lines. Note that the observed Y variables appear first, followed by the observed X variables. In our example, the original data already were in the correct order; hence, the SE line is not necessary. The next line of the LISREL program is the model line, and it appears as follows:

```
MO NX=6 NY=3 NK=2 NE=1 LX=FU LY=FU TD=SY TE=SY BE=FU GA=FU PS=SY PH=SY
```

MO is required and indicates that the line is the model line. NX is the number of *observed* X variables, NY is the number of *observed* Y variables, NK is the number of *latent* X variables, and NE is the number of *latent* Y variables. (In LISREL, latent X variables are called Ksi variables—hence the use of NK—and latent Y variables are called Eta variables—hence the use of NE.) The remainder of the model line will be explained later. The order in which these elements of the MO line are specified is arbitrary; they can be placed in any order. The MO line must appear after the lines mentioned above and before the lines discussed below.

Following the model line is a set of lines that provide labels for the latent variables. They are:

```
LK
Mother Father
LE
Child
```

The first line, LK, indicates that labels for the latent X variables will follow. The labels are then provided, separated by a blank, and limited to eight characters each. We adopt the convention of specifying latent variable labels with lowercase letters and observed variables in uppercase letters. This helps to keep the two distinct in the output. The line LE indicates that labels for the latent Y variables will be on the following line. This yields the following program, thus far:

```
ANALYSIS OF CHILD ACHIEVEMENT
DA NO=278 NI=9
LA
C1 C2 C3 M1 M2 M3 F1 F2 F3
CM FI = CHILD.DAT
MO NX=6 NY=3 NK=2 NE=1 LX=FU LY=FU TD=SY TE=SY BE=FU GA=FU PS=SY PH=SY
LK
Mother Father
LE
Child
```

Models are communicated to LISREL using eight matrices. This may seem cumbersome, but the process is straightforward. Each matrix refers to a different part of the diagram in Figure 1.4. For example, one matrix refers to the causal paths from the latent X variables to the latent Y variables. Another matrix refers to the causal paths from the latent X variables to the indicators of the latent X variables, and so on. Our programming strategy requires us to specify the *pattern* of each matrix, using a PA line (which is explained shortly).

The Lambda X Matrix

This matrix focuses on the paths going from the latent X variables to the observed X variables. The matrix has latent X variables as columns and observed X variables as rows, with either a 1 or a 0 as an entry. The matrix in our example appears as follows:

	Mother	Father
M1	1	0
M2	1	0
M3	1	0
F1	0	1
F2	0	1
F3	0	1

A 1 appears in a given cell if there is a causal arrow in the path diagram going from the latent variable to the observed measure. For example, a 1 appears in the cell for M1 and

Mother because there is a causal arrow going from the latent variable Mother to the observed measure M1. A 0 appears in a cell if there is no causal arrow going from the latent variable to the observed measure. A 0 means to "fix" the path at 0 rather than estimate the path. The pattern of the Lambda X matrix is conveyed in LISREL using the following lines:

```
PA LX
1 0
1 0
1 0
0 1
0 1
0 1
```

The first line has a PA to indicate that pattern data are to follow, and the LX identifies the matrix that the data describes (LX stands for Lambda X).

The Lambda Y Matrix

The Lambda Y (LY) matrix focuses on the paths going from the latent Y variables to the observed Y variables. The matrix has latent Y variables as columns and observed Y variables as rows, with either a 1 or a 0 as an entry. The matrix in our example appears as follows:

	Child
C1	1
C2	1
C3	1

As with the Lambda X matrix, a 1 appears in a given cell if there is a causal arrow in the path diagram going from the latent variable to the observed measure. A 0 appears in a cell if there is no causal arrow going from the latent variable to the observed measure.

The Theta Delta Matrix

The Theta Delta (TD) matrix focuses on measurement error (the e variables in Figure 1.4) for the observed X variables. It is a variance-covariance matrix between the e scores. It is always a square, symmetric matrix. Thus, if there are six e scores, TD will be a 6×6 matrix. If there were only three e scores, TD would be a 3×3 matrix. Because the matrix is symmetric, it is redundant to specify the entire matrix. Once we have specified the lower triangle of the matrix, we know what the upper triangle must be. That is why we specify TD = SY (SY stands for symmetric) on the model line (i.e., we intend to specify a pattern only for the lower triangle of the matrix).

The matrix lists the six e scores associated with the X variables as columns and the same six e scores as rows. The cell entries are either 1 or 0. In our example:

	e_4	e_5	e_6	e_7	e_8	e_9
e_4	1					
e_5	0	1				
e_6	0	0	1			
e_7	0	0	0	1		
e_8	0	0	0	0	1	
e_9	0	0	0	0	0	1

The diagonal elements of the matrix, all the 1s, represent error variance and correspond to measurement error. A 1 indicates that we want to estimate how much error variance there is in the measure. The off-diagonal elements represent correlated errors. A 0 means that the two error scores are not correlated (i.e., the correlations are "fixed" at 0), whereas an entry of 1 means that the two error scores are correlated and that the size of this covariance is to be estimated. In this example, none of the error scores is assumed to be correlated with any of the others.

The Theta Epsilon Matrix

The Theta Epsilon (TE) matrix focuses on measurement error (the e variables in Figure 1.4) for the observed Y variables. It is identical in form to the Theta Delta matrix, but the focus is on Y scores rather than X scores. It too is always a square, symmetric matrix. Thus, if there are three e scores for the Y variables, TE will be a 3×3 matrix. In our example, there are three e scores associated with Y variables; hence, the Theta Epsilon matrix is a 3×3 matrix:

	e_1	e_2	e_3
e_1	1		
e_2	0	1	
e_3	0	0	1

We indicate through this pattern matrix that we want to estimate the error variances for the Y measures and that none of the errors is correlated with any of the others.

The Phi Matrix

The Phi (PH) matrix is a variance-covariance matrix for the latent X variables. It is always symmetrical (see the MO line above). If there are two latent X variables, PH will be a 2×2 matrix. If there are four latent X variables, PH will be a 4×4 matrix. In our example, there are two latent X variables, and these appear in the columns and the rows:

	Mother	Father
Mother	1	
Father	1	1

As with the other symmetric matrices, we enter only the lower triangle of the matrix. A 1 means to estimate the parameter, and a 0 means to "fix" it at 0. The 1s in the diagonal tell LISREL to estimate the variance of the latent X variables. This will always be necessary for the examples considered in this monograph. The reason these variances are estimated is explained later in this chapter. The 1 in the off-diagonal element indicates that the two latent X variables are expected to be correlated. This typically also will be the case. Thus, the most common form of the Phi matrix is a series of 1s arranged in lower triangular form. If the off-diagonal element had been specified as 0, then LISREL would derive parameter estimates under the constraint that mother and father achievement have a 0 covariance.

The Gamma Matrix

The Gamma (GA) matrix specifies the causal paths from the latent X variables to the latent Y variables. The latent X variables are listed as columns, and the latent Y variables are rows:

	Mother	*Father*
Child	1	1

A 1 appears if there is a causal path going from the column variable to the row variable. If there is no such causal path, then a 0 appears.

The Beta Matrix

The Beta (BE) matrix specifies causal paths among different latent Y variables. The latent Y variables are listed as columns and the latent Y variables are also listed as rows. A 1 appears in a cell of the matrix if the column variable in question influences the row variable. Otherwise a 0 appears. A latent Y variable can never directly influence itself; hence, this matrix always has 0s in the diagonal. In our example, we have only a single latent Y variable (Child), so that the PA statement for this matrix has a 0 following it:

	Child
Child	0

The Psi Matrix

The Psi (PS) matrix focuses on the latent residual terms, E, in the path diagram. These E variables occur only for latent Y constructs. The PS matrix is a variance-covariance matrix and is symmetric in form (see the MO line). The different E scores are listed as columns, and these same E scores are listed as rows. The diagonals are typically set to 1 to indicate that we want to estimate the latent error variance. The off-diagonal elements are used to indicate correlated residuals. In our example, there is only a single E score. Psi is thus a 1×1 matrix with a 1 in the diagonal:

These patterns for the eight matrices are added to the initial program, yielding the following program code:[2]

```
ANALYSIS OF CHILD ACHIEVEMENT
DA NO=278 NI=9
LA
C1 C2 C3 M1 M2 M3 F1 F2 F3
CM FI = CHILD.DAT
MO NX=6 NY=3 NK=2 NE=1 LX=FU LY=FU TD=SY TE=SY BE=FU GA=FU PS=SY PH=SY
LK
Mother Father
LE
Child
PA LX
1 0
1 0
1 0
0 1
0 1
0 1
PA LY
1
1
1
PA TD
1
0 1
0 0 1
0 0 0 1
0 0 0 0 1
0 0 0 0 0 1
PA TE
1
0 1
0 0 1
PA PH
1
1 1
PA GA
1 1
PA BE
0
PA PS
1
```

Specifying the Metric of Latent Variables

Although the entire model has now been conveyed to LISREL, there is still an additional detail. Latent variables are unobserved and, consequently, they have no metric. For example, is the latent variable Mother scored on a scale of 1 to 10, 1 to 100, or −3 to +3? The metric of the latent variable Mother needs to be defined. This typically is done by assigning a metric from one of the indicators of the latent variable. For example, we might tell LISREL to use a metric that is the same as the metric for variable M1. In this case, M1 would be called a *reference* variable or reference indicator. Every latent variable must have a reference variable so that the latent variable has a defined metric.[3] The following program lines accomplish this:

```
FI LX(1,1) LX(4,2), LY(1,1)
VA 1.0 LX(1,1) LX(4,2) LY(1,1)
```

The first line isolates the cell in the Lambda X matrix (or the Lambda Y matrix) that corresponds to the reference variable to be used. LX(1,1) refers to the first row and the first column of the Lambda X matrix, LX(4,2) refers to the fourth row and second column of the Lambda X matrix, and LY(1,1) refers to the first row and the first column of the Lambda Y matrix. Thus, M1 will be used as a reference variable for Mother. This latent variable can be thought of (crudely) as ranging from 1 to 10, in the same fashion as M1. F1 is used as a reference variable for Father, and C1 is used as a reference variable for Child. The FI command tells LISREL to "fix" (rather than estimate) all the paths listed on the FI line. LISREL assumes the fix value to be 0 unless specifically instructed to do otherwise, using a value specified on the VA line, where VA stands for "Value." The VA line lists all the cells from the previous line. The two lines taken together have the effect of fixing the path coefficient from the relevant latent variables to the observed variables at 1.0. It is this set of operations that creates the reference variables. Again, all latent variables, both X and Y, must have a reference variable in order to define their metric. Without the reference variables (also called "reference indicators"), LISREL does not know on what "scale" the latent variables are "measured." The choice of a reference indicator can be critical, and issues in the selection of such measures are discussed in Chapters 2 and 5.

The final line is the output line, which indicates what we want to print out. It has the general form:

```
OU SC RS MI
```

The OU line is mandatory. SC tells LISREL to print a (completely) standardized solution, RS requests a residual analysis, and MI requests modification indices (see Appendix A). The complete program code is:

```
ANALYSIS OF CHILD ACHIEVEMENT
DA NO=278 NI=9
LA
C1 C2 C3 M1 M2 M3 F1 F2 F3
```

```
CM FI = CHILD.DAT
MO NX=6 NY=3 NK=2 NE=1 LX=FU LY=FU TD=SY TE=SY BE=FU GA=FU PS=SY PH=SY
LK
Mother Father
LE
Child
PA LX              !      Mother Father
1 0                ! M1
1 0                ! M2
1 0                ! M3
0 1                ! F1
0 1                ! F2
0 1                ! F3
PA LY              !         Child
1                  ! C1
1                  ! C2
1                  ! C3
PA TD              !      M1 M2 M3 F1 F2 F3
1                  ! M1
0 1                ! M2
0 0 1              ! M3
0 0 0 1            ! F1
0 0 0 0 1          ! F2
0 0 0 0 0 1        ! F3
PA TE              !      C1 C2 C3
1                  ! C1
0 1                ! C2
0 0 1              ! C3
PA PH              !         Mother Father
1                  ! Mother
1 1                ! Father
PA GA              !         Mother Father
1 1                ! Child
PA BE              !         Child
0                  ! Child
PA PS              !         Child
1                  ! Child
FI LX(1,1) LX(4,2), LY(1,1)      ! Set reference indicators
VA 1.0 LX(1,1) LX(4,2) LY(1,1)   ! Set reference indicators
OU SC RS MI
```

This program illustrates an additional feature of LISREL. When LISREL encounters an exclamation point, it assumes that everything that follows on the line is a comment (except for a semicolon, which terminates the comment). These comments can be used to annotate programs, making it easier to follow the logic of the program. We will use these comments, or remark lines, to identify the contents of the columns and rows of a matrix. The columns are annotated on the PA line, and the rows are annotated on separate lines directly beneath the PA line.

In the chapters that follow, we will also number the lines of the program, in order to facilitate commentary. The line numbers do not actually appear in the LISREL program code and should not be included when you are writing programs. We can also now clarify the remaining parameters on the MO line. On this line, we list each matrix for which we intend to specify a set of PA lines. The acronym SY means the matrix is symmetric, and the acronym FU means that the matrix is "full," or not symmetric. It actually is not necessary to specify every matrix on the MO line, as LISREL has defaults for each matrix built into the program. This is also true of the various PA lines. We have found it to be a good practice, however, for beginning programmers to keep track of what matrices are being manipulated by explicitly stating them on the MO line and then following this with a set of PA lines for each matrix.

Program Output

An abbreviated output for the program appears in Table 1.1. Before considering the output, we must digress and consider an issue central to all structural equation modeling. In our example, we analyzed a 9×9 covariance matrix for the nine observed measures. We want to test whether the pattern of variances and covariances within this matrix can be accounted for by the model in Figure 1.4, or, stated another way, whether the patterning of variances and covariances is consistent with the model in Figure 1.4. LISREL performs a number of "goodness-of-fit" tests to evaluate the compatibility of an a priori specified model (such as that in Figure 1.4) and the observed sample data. If the model is consistent with the data, then it makes sense to examine path coefficients and parameter estimates of the model. If a model is not consistent with the sample data, then it should be rejected accordingly.

LISREL provides more than 15 different indices of goodness of fit that reflect the consistency between a model and the covariance data. The choice of a fit index to use when evaluating the viability of a model is controversial. Current thought is that multiple fit indices should be considered (see Bollen & Long, 1993). A brief discussion of relevant issues is presented in Appendix A, along with further development of the issue of comparing predicted and observed covariances. We focus here only on a single fit index, namely the traditional chi-square test of fit. Although we strongly recommend that additional fit indices be considered, the focus on the chi-square test is sufficient to illustrate the logic of our approach throughout this monograph.

The chi-square test is a test of perfect model fit in which the null hypothesis is that the model fits the population data perfectly. A statistically significant chi-square causes rejection of the null hypothesis, implying imperfect model fit and possible rejection of the model. A statistically nonsignificant chi-square is consistent with a good model fit and suggests that the model can be retained as viable. Note that this situation is reversed from traditional hypothesis testing situations, in which the null hypothesis is typically that of "no effect" or "no relationship" between variables. The LISREL output in Table 1.1 yielded a chi-square value of 18.72 with 24 degrees of freedom, which is statistically nonsignificant. This is consistent with a viable model.

Turning to the output in Table 1.1, we can gain a sense of the measurement error influencing each of our observed measures by examining the output labeled LISREL

TABLE 1.1
Abbreviated LISREL Output

GOODNESS-OF-FIT STATISTICS

    CHI-SQUARE WITH 24 DEGREES OF FREEDOM = 18.72 (P = 0.77)

LISREL ESTIMATES (MAXIMUM LIKELIHOOD)

    SQUARED MULTIPLE CORRELATIONS FOR Y - VARIABLES

        C1   C2   C3
      ------ ------ ------
       0.94   0.93   0.96

    SQUARED MULTIPLE CORRELATIONS FOR X - VARIABLES

        M1   M2   M3   F1   F2   F3
      ------ ------ ------ ------ ------ ------
       0.80   0.84   0.87   0.83   0.83   0.81

    SQUARED MULTIPLE CORRELATIONS FOR STRUCTURAL EQUATIONS

        Child

       0.70

    GAMMA

        Mother Father
        ------ ------
Child   1.03   1.09
        (0.08) (0.08)
        13.31   14.54

COMPLETELY STANDARDIZED SOLUTION

    CORRELATION MATRIX OF ETA AND KSI

          Child   Mother Father
         ------ ------ ------
Child   1.00
Mother   0.59   1.00
Father   0.64   0.07   1.00

ESTIMATES and the subsection called SQUARED MULTIPLE CORRELATIONS FOR Y - VARIABLES and SQUARED MULTIPLE CORRELATIONS FOR X - VARIABLES. Each observed variable is listed with a value beneath it that corresponds to the estimated proportion of variance that is *not* the result of measurement error (i.e., the value of the reliability coefficient). For example, 94% of the variance in C1 results from the latent variable Child and 6% is the result of other factors (measurement error). The latent variable Child explains 93% of the variance in C2; the remaining 7% is attributable to measurement error. In the subsection of LISREL ESTIMATES called SQUARED MULTIPLE CORRELATIONS FOR STRUCTURAL EQUATIONS is the estimated squared multiple correlation for predicting the latent criterion variable from the latent predictors, having adjusted for measurement error. In our example, the value is 0.70, indicating that mother achievement and father achievement account for 70% of the variance of child achievement.

In the section called GAMMA is the regression equation of interest, minus an intercept term. Although it is possible to estimate intercepts in LISREL, they typically are of lesser theoretical interest than are slopes and therefore are not considered here. The unstandardized regression coefficient appears beneath each latent variable. Directly beneath the coefficient is the estimated standard error and a z test of statistical significance. If the absolute value of z is greater than 1.96 (using an alpha of 0.05), then the coefficient is statistically significant. For mother achievement orientation, the unstandardized regression coefficient is 1.03 and is statistically significant ($z = 13.31$, $p < 0.05$). For every one unit that mother achievement increases, child achievement is predicted to increase 1.03 units, using the metrics of the reference variables, M1 and C1. For father achievement orientation, the unstandardized regression coefficient is 1.09 and is statistically significant ($z = 14.54$, $p < 0.05$). For every one unit that father achievement increases, child achievement is predicted to increase 1.09 units, using the metric of the reference variables, F1 and C1. These coefficients are estimated coefficients taking into account measurement error (i.e., the error theory represented in Figure 1.4). They are superior to traditional least squares estimates because the latter estimates are biased by measurement error. Finally, in the section called COMPLETELY STANDARDIZED SOLUTION, the estimated correlations between all the latent variables are presented in the subsection called CORRELATION MATRIX OF ETA AND KSI.

Path Diagrams as Linear Equations

The path diagram in Figure 1.4, as with any path diagram, can be translated into a series of linear regression equations. These equations are the cornerstone of the LISREL analysis. One equation focuses on the latent variables alone. In Figure 1.4, the latent Y variable (child achievement) is the dependent variable and is said to be a linear function of the two latent X variables (mother achievement and father achievement). The formal regression equation, using sample notation, is

$$CA = a + b_1 MA + b_2 FA + E \qquad (1.3)$$

where CA is the latent variable of child achievement, MA is the latent variable of mother achievement, FA is the latent variable of father achievement, E is a residual term, a is the intercept, and b_1 and b_2 are regression (i.e., path) coefficients. This equation is often referred to as a *structural model* because it focuses on the structural relations between latent variables. In LISREL, the form of this equation is specified using the Gamma matrix, the Beta matrix, and the Psi matrix. Note that none of these matrices includes an intercept term. The intercept usually is not of substantive interest and is not directly estimated in most LISREL applications. There are cases in which the intercept will be estimated, examples of which are presented in Chapter 4.

In addition to the structural model, there is a *measurement model* that also is expressed in the form of linear equations. Each observed measure is said to be a linear function of its underlying latent variable plus measurement error. For example, the formal regression equation for the observed measure C1 in Figure 1.4 is (using sample notation):

$$C1 = a_{C1} + b_{C1}CA + e_1 \qquad (1.4)$$

where C1 is the observed measure, CA is the latent variable of child achievement, a_{C1} is an intercept term, b_{C1} is the regression (i.e., path) coefficient, and e_1 is the residual. There is a separate regression equation for each observed measure. In Figure 1.4, there are nine such equations. The various b coefficients from these "measurement equations" are specified in LISREL using the Lambda X and Lambda Y matrices, and the various e terms are specified using the Theta Delta and Theta Epsilon matrices. The intercept terms, again, usually are not of substantive interest, but we will consider them formally in Chapter 4.

It can be seen, then, that the model in Figure 1.4 actually has 10 linear equations underlying it, a single structural equation and nine measurement equations. LISREL obtains simultaneous estimates of the population coefficients for the 10 equations (as well as parameters focused on error variance, correlated predictors, and other features of the model) using estimation methods that are distinct from traditional multiple regression analysis (see Appendix A). This, in part, is because the predictor variables in every equation are latent variables, which are not directly measured (as is the case with predictor variables in traditional multiple regression).

Statistical Assumptions of Multiple Regression and Structural Equation Analysis

In this monograph, we will formally compare traditional multiple regression analysis of interaction effects with approaches that rely on structural equation modeling with multiple indicators and maximum likelihood estimation. It will be helpful to make explicit the statistical assumptions of the two approaches. Traditional least squares estimation using Equation 1.1 makes the following assumptions about the population data from which sample data are randomly selected:

1. The expected value of the residual term is 0.
2. There is no serial correlation (or dependency) between residuals.

3. The residuals exhibit constant variance (homoscedasticity) across values of the predicted Y scores.

4. The covariance between the predicted Y scores and the residual scores is 0.

5. There is not complete multicollinearity among predictors.

When these assumptions are satisfied, an ordinary least squares (OLS) estimator is said to be the best linear, unbiased estimator (BLUE), and it has minimum variance in the class of all linear, unbiased estimators (see Berry, 1993, for elaboration of these assumptions).

Although it is not a formal assumption of the estimation procedure, applications of traditional regression are predicated on the assumption that the measures used in the analysis are not fallible, that is, that there is no measurement error in them. The presence of measurement error means that the observed scores do not correspond to the true scores underlying the constructs in question, and this can produce bias in the estimates of the regression coefficients associated with the true scores. It is these "true score" coefficients that are of primary interest in theory testing. The presence of bias in their estimation is problematic.

Traditional maximum likelihood estimation using a multiple-indicator, structural equation model (SEM) approach also makes assumptions about the structure of the population data. Stated in their most restrictive form, the estimation methods assume that the measures used to assess both the predictor and criterion variables are multivariately normally distributed. Residuals are also assumed to be serially independent, homoscedastic, and unrelated to relevant exogenous predictors, as well as having a mean of 0 (see Bollen, 1989, for elaboration). Under such constraints, maximum likelihood estimators of regression coefficients have the following properties:

1. they are asymptotically unbiased,
2. they are consistent estimators,
3. they are asymptotically efficient, and
4. they are asymptotically normally distributed.

Effective estimation also requires the absence of complete multicollinearity among predictors as well as positive definite input matrices and matrices of predicted covariances (see Appendix A). When sample sizes are small, these properties do not necessarily hold.

Although multivariate normality among measures is desirable, there exist scenarios in which maximum likelihood (ML) estimators have excellent properties even when the data are not multivariately normally distributed. For example, ML estimators are consistent even when the population distribution is not multivariate normal. This means that as the sample size becomes increasingly large, the sample estimators eventually converge onto the values of the population parameters (although tests of statistical significance may not be valid). Maximum likelihood estimators retain all four properties mentioned above, even when nonnormality exists, under the following set of conditions:

1. the residual terms within an SEM model are multivariate normally distributed (each with a mean of 0) and have constant variance across relevant combinations of the predictors,

2. the residuals are not serially correlated (i.e., are independent) and are independent of the relevant predictors, and

3. the distribution of the observed measures does not depend on the population Beta, Gamma, or Psi coefficients (see Bollen, 1989; Johnston, 1984).

Similarly, if the exogenous variables are fixed rather than random, then the assumption of multivariate normality with respect to the fixed exogenous variables can be relaxed without adversely affecting estimation.

Traditional multiple regression analysis actually is a special case of the SEM approach. Specifically, multiple regression can be cast as the analysis of latent variables with single indicators, where random measurement errors are constrained to 0 and perfect correspondence is assumed between the latent and observed measures. Under these conditions, an SEM (maximum likelihood) representation of multiple regression will produce identical results to OLS estimation. SEM approaches diverge from traditional regression when multiple indicators of a construct are introduced and "overidentified" models are evaluated (see Appendix A).

Notes

1. We often refer to "moderator" variables that moderate the impact of one variable on another. This implies an asymmetry of the interaction effect, which is imposed at the level of theory. Statistically, traditional product term analysis is based on symmetric interactions (see Jaccard, Turrisi, & Wan, 1990).

2. There are additional matrices for LISREL programming that focus on latent variable means and intercepts as well as correlated measurement errors between the observed X and observed Y variables (the TH matrix). These are discussed either in Chapter 4 or in Jöreskog and Sorbom (1993).

3. There are exceptions, but they are not relevant for our purposes.

2. QUALITATIVE MODERATOR VARIABLES

Researchers frequently encounter situations in which they are interested in interaction effects involving a moderator variable, either qualitative or quantitative, with few values. Analyses of these types of interactions are accomplished using the "multigroup" strategy in LISREL, the primary topic of this chapter. Consider the following example. A group of individuals watched a televised debate between two presidential candidates. After viewing the debate, the individuals completed a set of rating scales indicating the extent to which they thought the Democratic candidate won the debate. Three different scales were used and served as indicators of judged success in winning. The first indicator, S1, was a rating scale that ranged from 0 to 20. The other two indicators, S2

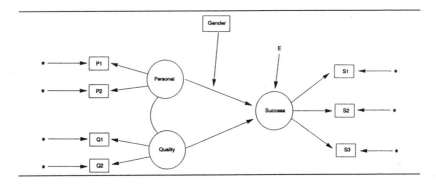

Figure 2.1. Multiple-Indicator Path Model for Effects of Perceived Personableness and Perceived Quality of Arguments on Judged Success in a Debate

and S3, were multi-item scales that ranged from 0 to 25. In all cases, higher scores implied higher success judgments.

The individuals also rated how personable the candidate was as well as how convincing her arguments were. Two indicators of each construct were obtained. The two ratings for personableness, P1 and P2, were both semantic differential type scales ranging from 1 to 7, with higher scores indicating greater perceived personableness. The two ratings for the quality of arguments, Q1 and Q2, also were 7-point semantic differential scales, with higher scores indicating higher perceived quality of the arguments.

The investigator was interested in the path model in Figure 2.1. In this model, the latent variable of judged success is regressed onto the latent variables of personableness and argument quality. The investigator hypothesized that the strength of the path from the latent variable of personableness to judged success would differ as a function of gender. Specifically, the investigator theorized that this path would be stronger for females than for males. Thus, there is a hypothesized interaction between gender and the perceived personableness of the candidate as determinants of judged success in winning the debate. Gender is the moderator variable (Z), judged success is the criterion (Y), and perceived personableness and perceived quality of arguments are the predictor variables (X_1 and X_2).

Nested Goodness of-Fit Strategy

In order to test the interaction effect, two steps are required. The first step involves a "multiple-group" solution in which LISREL derives parameter estimates for each group separately as well as a measure of goodness of fit of the model for both groups considered simultaneously. The overall test of goodness of fit is based on a pooling of the fit measures from each group separately. A statistically nonsignificant pooled chi-square is consistent with a model that fits well across groups. A statistically significant pooled chi-square implies poor model fit in at least one of the groups. Before proceeding to step 2, one must have a model that fits well at step 1.

The step 1 analysis does not formally evaluate the interaction effect. Rather, it provides perspectives on how well the model fits the data when LISREL is permitted to estimate coefficients in each group separately and without constraints across groups. Suppose that there is no interaction effect and that the path coefficients for the influence of personableness on judged success are, in fact, identical for males and females. This suggests that any difference in the sample regression (path) coefficients for males versus females is due to sampling error. Now suppose we re-estimate the model but this time impose an equality constraint on the solution. Specifically, we permit LISREL to fit the data as best it can using the model as a framework, but now with the constraint that the regression coefficients for judged success on personableness be equal in the two groups. If there is indeed no interaction effect and the two path coefficients are equal in the populations, then such a constraint should not adversely affect model fit relative to the analysis in step 1. If there is a reasonably sizable interaction effect, then such a constraint will adversely affect model fit. Step 2 involves such a constrained solution. The results are then compared to the unconstrained solution in step 1. In sum, we perform the following operations:

1. Calculate model fit (e.g., by means of a chi-square test) using a multiple-group solution in which LISREL estimates parameters in different groups with no across-group constraints.
2. Calculate model fit (e.g., by means of a chi-square test) using a multiple-group solution in which LISREL estimates parameters in different groups with an across-group constraint imposed to reflect the interaction effect.
3. Calculate the difference in model fit by comparing the fit index for the constrained solution with the fit index for the unconstrained solution. Based on the size of this difference (relative to 0), make a conclusion about the interaction effect (using the procedures described below).

To accomplish step 1, the LISREL programming strategy in Chapter 1 is used, but separate programs are written for males and females and then stacked onto one another. Here is the program code:

```
LINE
001    MALES - GROUP 1
002    DA NG=2 NO=154 NI=7
003    LA
004    S1 S2 S3 P1 P2 Q1 Q2
005    CM FI = MALE.DAT
006    MO NX=4 NY=3 NK=2 NE=1 LX=FU LY=FU TD=SY TE=SY BE=FU GA=FU
       PS=SY PH=SY
007    LK
008    Person Quality
```

```
009    LE
010    Success
011    PA LX              !           Person Quality
012    1 0                !  P1
013    1 0                !  P2
014    0 1                !  Q1
015    0 1                !  Q2
016    PA LY              !           Success
017    1                  !  S1
018    1                  !  S2
019    1                  !  S3
020    PA TD              !           P1 P2 Q1 Q2
021    1                  !  P1
022    0 1                !  P2
023    0 0 1              !  Q1
024    0 0 0 1            !  Q2
025    PA TE              !           S1 S2 S3
026    1                  !  S1
027    0 1                !  S2
028    0 0 1              !  S3
029    PA PH              !           Person Quality
030    1                  !  Person
031    1 1                !  Quality
032    PA GA              !           Person Quality
033    1 1                !  Success
034    PA BE              !           Success
035    0                  !  Success
036    PA PS              !           Success
037    1                  !  Success
038    FI LX(1,1) LX(3,2) LY(1,1)      ! Set reference indicators
039    VA 1.0 LX(1,1) LX(3,2) LY(1,1)  ! Set reference indicators
040    OU SC RS MI
041    FEMALES - GROUP 2
042    DA NO=125
043    LA
044    S1 S2 S3 P1 P2 Q1 Q2
045    CM FI = FEMALE.DAT
046    MO NX=4 NY=3 NK=2 NE=1 LX=FU LY=FU TD=SY TE=SY BE=FU GA=FU
       PS=SY PH=SY
047    LK
048    Person Quality
049    LE
050    Success
051    PA LX              !           Person Quality
052    1 0                !  P1
053    1 0                !  P2
054    0 1                !  Q1
055    0 1                !  Q2
056    PA LY              !           Success
```

```
057   1                   !    S1
058   1                   !    S2
059   1                   !    S3
060   PA TD               !         P1 P2 Q1 Q2
061   1                   !    P1
062   0 1                 !    P2
063   0 0 1               !    Q1
064   0 0 0 1             !    Q2
065   PA TE               !         S1 S2 S3
066   1                   !    S1
067   0 1                 !    S2
068   0 0 1               !    S3
069   PA PH               !         Person  Quality
070   1                   !    Person
071   1 1                 !    Quality
072   PA GA               !         Person  Quality
073   1 1                 !    Success
074   PA BE               !         Success
075   0                   !    Success
076   PA PS               !         Success
077   1                   !    Success
078   FI LX(1,1) LX(3,2) LY(1,1)      ! Set reference indicators
079   VA 1.0 LX(1,1) LX(3,2) LY(1,1)  ! Set reference indicators
080   OU SC RS MI
```

The stacked programs for the two groups are identical, with three exceptions. First, the title lines (001 and 041) are different, in order to differentiate the groups. Second, the input file on the CM lines (005 and 045) are different for the two groups, indicating the different files where the data are located. Third, the DA line for the first group (line 002) has an extra specification, namely NG=2. NG stands for "number of groups" and tells LISREL how many "stacked programs" or groups there are. This line also specifies the sample size for the first group. Line 042 is the corresponding DA line for the second group. It specifies only the sample size for the second group. LISREL assumes that the number of input variables (NI) is the same as that specified on the DA line for the first group (line 002).[1]

The LISREL output presents the parameter estimates for each group separately and the chi-square for the overall model fit just after the last group. The overall chi-square from the analysis was 15.25 with 22 degrees of freedom, which is statistically nonsignificant. This is consistent with good model fit across the groups. The "step 2" program is identical to the program for step 1 with one exception. An "equality constraint" line is added just before the OU line of the last group (line 080):

```
EQ GA(1,1,1) GA(2,1,1)
```

This line signifies to LISREL that it is to impose a constraint when deriving parameter estimates. The constraint is that all path coefficients listed after EQ must equal one another. GA indicates that the equality constraint applies to the Gamma matrix, which is where the path coefficient of interest is located. The first value in the parentheses refers to the group number, the second value refers to the row number, and the third value refers to the column number. Thus, we are telling LISREL to constrain the cell corresponding to the first row and first column of the Gamma matrix for group 1 to equal the cell corresponding to the first row and the first column of the Gamma matrix for group 2. This is the path coefficient of theoretical interest.

The resulting chi-square for the program with this equality constraint added is 29.80 with 23 degrees of freedom. The difference in the chi-squares for step 2 minus step 1 is 29.80 − 15.25 = 14.55. As it turns out, this difference also is distributed as a chi-square statistic with degrees of freedom equal to the difference between the step 2 and step 1 degrees of freedom, namely, 23 − 22 = 1. A chi-square of 14.55 with 1 degree of freedom is statistically significant, suggesting that the difference in model fit is statistically significant. An interaction effect is present, because making the assumption of no interaction (i.e., equal slopes for males and females) significantly adversely affects model fit.

The path coefficients from the Gamma matrix under LISREL ESTIMATES in the step 1 analysis provide the estimates of the regression coefficients for males and females. For males, the path coefficient from the latent variable of personableness to success was 0.95, whereas for females, the corresponding path coefficient was 1.88. The difference between the path coefficients is statistically significant because of the nested fit test. The impact of perceived personableness on judged success was stronger for females than for males.

The general multigroup strategy with nested goodness-of-fit tests can be conducted for any number of groups using any combination of constraints. For example, here is the program for introducing equality constraints for the path from personableness to success for three different ethnic groups (a step 2 analysis):

```
LINE
001     AFRICAN AMERICANS - GROUP 1
002     DA NG=3 NO=102 NI=7
003     LA
004     S1 S2 S3 P1 P2 Q1 Q2
005     CM FI= BLACK.DAT
006     MO NX=4 NY=3 NK=2 NE=1 LX=FU LY=FU TD=SY TE=SY BE=FU GA=FU
        PS=SY PH=SY
007     LK
008     Person Quality
009     LE
010     Success
011     PA LX              !            Person Quality
012     1  0               !    P1
013     1  0               !    P2
014     0  1               !    Q1
015     0  1               !    Q2
016     PA LY              !            Success
017     1                  !    S1
018     1                  !    S2
019     1                  !    S3
```

```
020    PA TD              !            P1 P2 Q1 Q2
021    1                  !    P1
022    0 1                !    P2
023    0 0 1              !·   Q1
024    0 0 0 1            !    Q2
025    PA TE              !            S1 S2 S3
026    1                  !    S1
027    0 1                !    S2
028    0 0 1              !    S3
029    PA PH              !            Person Quality
030    1                  !    Person
031    1 1                !    Quality
032    PA GA              !            Person Quality
033    1 1                !    Success
034    PA BE              !            Success
035    0                  !    Success
036    PA PS              !            Success
037    1                  !    Success
038    FI LX(1,1) LX(3,2) LY(1,1)      ! Set reference indicators
039    VA 1.0 LX(1,1) LX(3,2) LY(1,1)  ! Set reference indicators
040    OU SC RS MI
041    HISPANICS - GROUP 2
042    DA NO=100 NI=7
043    LA
044    S1 S2 S3 P1 P2 Q1 Q2
045    CM FI= HISP.DAT
046    MO NX=4 NY=3 NK=2 NE=1 LX=PS LY=PS TD=PS TE=PS BE=PS GA=PS
       PS=PS PH=PS
047    LK
048    Person Quality
049    LE
050    Success
051    OU SC RS MI
052    WHITES - GROUP 3
053    DA NO=101 NI=7
054    LA
055    S1 S2 S3 P1 P2 Q1 Q2
056    CM FI= WHITE.DAT
057    MO NX=4 NY=3 NK=2 NE=1 LX=PS LY=PS TD=PS TE=PS BE=PS GA=PS
       PS=PS PH=PS
058    LK
059    Person Quality
060    LE
061    Success
062    EQ GA(1,1,1) GA(2,1,1) GA(3,1,1)
063    OU SC RS MI
```

This program illustrates a programming shortcut. Instead of stacking an entire program for each of the groups following group 1, we delete all pattern matrices for the subsequent groups and change the MO line to refer to each matrix with the argument PS (see lines 046 and 057 as compared with line 006). This means to define the pattern of the matrix to be the same in format as the pattern matrix in the previous group (although the values of the estimated parameters within the matrix can vary across groups). The equality constraint occurs before the OU line in the last group (line 063) and imposes the constraint on all three groups.

The chi-square resulting from this program is compared with the chi-square test from a "step 1" analysis that uses the stacked program strategy for the three groups without any equality constraints. The step 1 chi-square was 44.96 ($df = 33$), and the step 2 chi-square was 64.16 ($df = 35$). The nested goodness-of-fit test yields a chi-square difference of 19.20 ($df = 2$), which is statistically significant, $p < 0.05$. This suggests that ethnicity moderates the impact of personableness on success judgments.

Exactly which pairs of groups among the three have significantly different path coefficients is determined by conducting nested chi-square tests between all possible pairs of groups (or a priori specified pairs), with a modified Bonferroni control for experimentwise Type I errors, if appropriate. For example, a test comparing the latent regression coefficients for groups 1 and 2 has this EQ line on line 062:

```
EQ GA(1,1,1) GA(2,1,1)
```

The resulting chi-square is contrasted with the chi-square with no constraints (i.e., from the step 1 analysis). In the present example, the chi-square for the constrained solution was 57.67 ($df = 34$), and the nested chi-square difference was 12.71 ($df = 1, p < 0.01$). A test comparing the latent regression coefficients for groups 1 and 3 would have the following EQ line on line 062:

```
EQ GA(1,1,1) GA(3,1,1)
```

The resulting chi-square for the above constrained solution was 46.59 ($df = 34$), and the nested chi-square difference was 1.63 ($df = 1, ns$). A test comparing groups 2 and 3 has the following EQ line on line 062:

```
EQ GA(2,1,1) GA(3,1,1)
```

The chi-square for this analysis is contrasted with the chi-square test from step 1. The chi-square for the constrained solution was 56.91 ($df = 34$), and the nested chi-square difference is 11.95 ($df = 1, p < 0.01$).

The modified Bonferroni method that we recommend to control experimentwise error rates is based on Holm (1979; see also Holland & Copenhaver, 1988; Seaman, Levin, & Serlin, 1991). It is more powerful than traditional Bonferroni methods but adequately maintains experimentwise error rates at the desired alpha level (usually 0.05). It is applied as follows. First, a p value is obtained for each contrast by consulting a table for the chi-square distribution or using a computer program that provides p values for the chi-square distribution. These p values are based on the chi-square differences between the "step 2" and "step 1" programs that focused on the pairwise contrasts and represent the probability of observing the chi-square difference, assuming that the null hypothesis of no effect is true. The p values are then ordered from smallest to largest. Equal p values are ordered arbitrarily or using theoretical criteria. The largest difference (which has the smallest p value) is evaluated based on an alpha of $0.05/c$, where c is the total number of pairwise contrasts performed. If this leads to rejection of the null hypothesis, then the next largest difference is tested against $0.05/(c-1)$, the remaining number of comparisons. If this test leads to null hypothesis rejection, then the next largest difference is tested against an alpha level of $0.05/(c-2)$ and so on, until a nonsignificant difference is observed. In the present example, the p values and alpha levels are as follows:

Order (i)	Chi-square	p Value	$\alpha/(c-i+1)$	Contrast
1	12.71	0.0004	0.017	AA versus H
2	11.95	0.0008	0.025	H versus W
3	1.63	0.129	0.050	AA versus W

The difference in path coefficients between African Americans and Hispanics is statistically significant, as is the difference in path coefficients between whites and Hispanics.

Three-Way Interactions

It also is possible to analyze three-way interactions using the multiple-group strategy. Suppose the theorist thought that the moderating effects of gender on the personableness-success path coefficient differ as a function of whether the individual is a Democrat or a Republican. He or she reasons that because Republicans tend to be more traditional than Democrats, the gender differences in the path coefficients will be more likely to manifest themselves in Republicans than in Democrats. This three-way interaction is tested using the following strategy. First, a "step 1" analysis is performed in which the model in Figure 2.1 is estimated for the four groups (male Democrats, female Democrats, male Republicans, and female Republicans) without any across-group equality constraints. The program code appears as follows:

```
LINE
001    MALE DEMOCRATS
002    DA NG=4 NO=101 NI=7
003    LA
004    S1 S2 S3 P1 P2 Q1 Q2
005    CM FI= MALEDEM.DAT
006    MO NX=4 NY=3 NK=2 NE=1 LX=FU LY=FU TD=SY TE=SY BE=FU GA=FU
       PS=SY PH=SY
007    LK
008    Person Quality
009    LE
010    Success
```

```
011    PA LX              !              Person Quality
012    1 0                !   P1
013    1 0                !   P2
014    0 1                !   Q1
015    0 1                !   Q2
016    PA LY              !              Success
017    1                  !   S1
018    1                  !   S2
019    1                  !   S3
020    PA TD              !              P1 P2 Q1 Q2
021    1                  !   P1
022    0 1                !   P2
023    0 0 1              !   Q1
024    0 0 0 1            !   Q2
025    PA TE              !              S1 S2 S3
026    1                  !   S1
027    0 1                !   S2
028    0 0 1              !   S3
029    PA PH              !              Person Quality
030    1                  !   Person
031    1 1                !   Quality
032    PA GA              !              Person Quality
033    1 1                !   Success
034    PA BE              !              Success
035    0                  !   Success
036    PA PS              !              Success
037    1                  !   Success
038    FI LX(1,1) LX(3,2) LY(1,1)     ! Set reference indicators
039    VA 1.0 LX(1,1) LX(3,2) LY(1,1) ! Set reference indicators
040    OU SC RS MI
041    FEMALE DEMOCRATS
042    DA NO=101 NI=7
043    LA
044    S1 S2 S3 P1 P2 Q1 Q2
045    CM FI= FEMDEM.DAT
046    MO NX=4 NY=3 NK=2 NE=1 LX=PS LY=PS TD=PS TE=PS BE=PS GA=PS
       PS=PS PH=PS
047    LK
048    Person Quality
049    LE
050    Success
051    OU SC RS MI
052    MALE REPUBLICANS
053    DA NO=102 NI=7
054    LA
055    S1 S2 S3 P1 P2 Q1 Q2
056    CM FI= MALEREP.DAT
057    MO NX=4 NY=3 NK=2 NE=1 LX=PS LY=PS TD=PS TE=PS BE=PS GA=PS
       PS=PS PH=PS
058    LK
```

```
059     Person Quality
060     LE
061     Success
062     OU SC RS MI
063     FEMALE REPUBLICANS
064     DA NO=102 NI=7
065     LA
066     S1 S2 S3 P1 P2 Q1 Q2
067     CM FI= FEMREP.DAT
068     MO NX=4 NY=3 NK=2 NE=1 LX=PS LY=PS TD=PS TE=PS BE=PS GA=PS
        PS=PS PH=PS
069     LK
070     Person Quality
071     LE
072     Success
073     OU SC RS MI
```

The "step 2" program is identical, but with the following line added:

```
CO GA(1,1,1) - GA(2,1,1) = GA(3,1,1) - GA(4,1,1)
```

This constraint line is added just prior to the output line of the last group (i.e., after line 072). Because it involves an algebraic manipulation on parameters, a CO command is used rather than an EQ command. The CO line constrains the difference in path coefficients for Democrats to be equal to the difference in path coefficients for Republicans. If these differences are unequal, a three-way interaction is implied.

If model fit is significantly affected by the introduction of this constraint (e.g., if the difference in chi-squares between the step 1 and step 2 analyses is statistically significant), then a three-way interaction exists. In the present example, the chi-square for the constrained solution was 49.49 ($df = 45$), the chi-square for the unconstrained solution was 37.49 ($df = 44$), and the nested chi-square difference was 12.00 ($df = 1$), a result that is statistically significant ($p < 0.05$). The difference in path coefficients (obtained from the path coefficients estimated for each group from the step 1 solution) between males and females was -1.40 for Republicans, and the corresponding difference between path coefficients for Democrats was 0.10. The disparity between these differences is statistically significant, as reflected by the statistically significant nested chi-square statistic.

To test if the difference in path coefficients between males and females within the Republicans (-1.40) is statistically significantly different from 0, one would contrast a step 1 chi-square with a chi-square that resulted from a program that constrained these two paths to be equal. This would involve adding the following line before the OU line (line 073) of the step 1 program:

```
EQ GA(3,1,1) GA(4,1,1)
```

A statistically significant nested chi-square test would imply that the difference of -1.40 is statistically significant. The corresponding contrast for the Democrats would replace this EQ line with the following:

```
EQ GA(1,1,1) GA(2,1,1)
```

and the nested chi-square test is performed accordingly.

Some general rules about the use of the CO line should be noted: (a) only free parameters (not fixed parameters) should appear on the right-hand side of the equation; (b) implicit equations, in which the parameter on the left side of the equation also appears on the right side of the same equation, are not permitted; and (c) when there are multiple CO lines, parameters that are constrained on previous CO lines (i.e., the left side of the equation) should not appear on the right side of any CO line.[2]

Three-Way Interactions With More Than Two Groups

The analysis of three-way interactions is readily generalized to the case in which there are more than two groups being compared. For example, suppose that in addition to Democrats and Republicans, there was a group of Independents, yielding a 2 (gender) by 3 (party identification) factorial design. A step 1 program would be executed with no equality constraints by stacking the six group programs. The program code appears as follows:

```
LINE
001    MALE DEMOCRATS
002    DA NG=6 NO=101 NI=7
003    LA
004    S1 S2 S3 P1 P2 Q1 Q2
005    CM FI= MALEDEM.DAT
006    MO NX=4 NY=3 NE=1 NK=2 LX=FU LY=FU TD=SY TE=SY BE=FU GA=FU
       PS=SY PH=SY
007    LK
008    Person Quality
009    LE
010    Success
011    PA LX          !          Person Quality
012    1 0            !  P1
013    1 0            !  P2
014    0 1            !  Q1
015    0 1            !  Q2
016    PA LY          !          Success
017    1              !  S1
018    1              !  S2
019    1              !  S3
020    PA TD          !          P1 P2 Q1 Q2
021    1              !  P1
022    0 1            !  P2
023    0 0 1          !  Q1
024    0 0 0 1        !  Q2
025    PA TE          !          S1 S2 S3
026    1              !  S1
```

```
027   0 1                  !    S2
028   0 0 1                !    S3
029   PA PH                !              Person Quality
030   1                    !    Person
031   1 1                  !    Quality
032   PA GA                !              Person Quality
033   1 1                  !    Success
034   PA BE                !         Success
035   0                    !    Success
036   PA PS                !         Success
037   1                    !    Success
038   FI LX(1,1) LX(3,2) LY(1,1)      ! Set reference indicators
039   VA 1.0 LX(1,1) LX(3,2) LY(1,1)  ! Set reference indicators
040   OU SC RS MI
041   FEMALE DEMOCRATS
042   DA NO=101 NI=7
043   LA
044   S1 S2 S3 P1 P2 Q1 Q2
045   CM FI= FEMDEM.DAT
046   MO NX=4 NY=3 NE=1 NK=2 LX=PS LY=PS TD=PS TE=PS BE=PS GA=PS
      PS=PS PH=PS
047   LK
048   Person Quality
049   LE
050   Success
051   OU SC RS MI
052   MALE REPUBLICANS
053   DA NO=102 NI=7
054   LA
055   S1 S2 S3 P1 P2 Q1 Q2
056   CM FI= MALEREP.DAT
057   MO NX=4 NY=3 NE=1 NK=2 LX=PS LY=PS TD=PS TE=PS BE=PS GA=PS
      PS=PS PH=PS
058   LK
059   Person Quality
060   LE
061   Success
062   OU SC RS MI
063   FEMALE REPUBLICANS
064   DA NO=102 NI=7
065   LA
066   S1 S2 S3 P1 P2 Q1 Q2
067   CM FI= FEMREP.DAT
068   MO NX=4 NY=3 NE=1 NK=2 LX=PS LY=PS TD=PS TE=PS BE=PS GA=PS
      PS=PS PH=PS
069   LK
070   Person Quality
071   LE
072   Success
```

```
073    OU SC RS MI
074    MALE INDEPENDENTS
075    DA NO=125 NI=7
076    LA
077    S1 S2 S3 P1 P2 Q1 Q2
078    CM FI= MALEIND.DAT
079    MO NX=4 NY=3 NE=1 NK=2 LX=PS LY=PS TD=PS TE=PS BE=PS GA=PS
       PS=PS PH=PS
080    LK
081    Person Quality
082    LE
083    Success
084    OU SC RS MI
085    FEMALE INDEPENDENTS
086    DA NO=125 NI=7
087    LA
088    S1 S2 S3 P1 P2 Q1 Q2
089    CM FI = FEMIND.DAT
090    MO NX=4 NY=3 NE=1 NK=2 LX=PS LY=PS TD=PS TE=PS BE=PS GA=PS
       PS=PS PH=PS
091    LK
092    Person Quality
093    LE
094    Success
095    OU SC RS MI
```

The chi-square test statistic for this program was 64.10 ($df = 66$). Because of the way that LISREL imposes nonlinear constraints, there are ambiguities in the test of the overall interaction for designs that are larger than 2×2 factorials. Although an omnibus test can be problematic, it is typical in practice to decompose a statistically significant omnibus interaction effect into a series of 2×2 subcontrasts, with a Bonferroni-based control for the experimentwise error rate (e.g., Keppel, 1982). Therefore, a reasonable strategy is to move directly to the 2×2 subcontrasts, omitting the omnibus test. If any of the contrasts is statistically significant (using the Bonferroni-based control for experimentwise error rates), then an overall interaction effect is declared to exist. Indeed, the need to conduct an omnibus test first has been questioned in general, because the Bonferroni-based procedure provides appropriate experimentwise control independent of the omnibus test (Jaccard, Becker, & Wood, 1984).

The present design is a 2×3 factorial (two levels of gender by three levels of party identification), and there are three possible 2×2 subtables. Thus, we must perform three separate "step 2" programs. The first program focuses on the gender difference in path coefficients for Democrats versus Republicans and includes the following CO line before line 095:

```
CO GA(1,1,1) - GA(2,1,1) = GA(3,1,1) - GA(4,1,1)
```

The chi-square from this analysis is compared with the chi-square from the step 1 analysis using the nested goodness-of-fit test. A statistically significant chi-square difference implies gender differences in path coefficients for these two groups. In the present analysis, the constrained chi-square was 76.10 ($df = 67$), and the nested chi-square difference was 12.00 ($df = 1, p < 0.01$).

The second program focuses on the gender differences in path coefficients for Democrats and Independents and includes the following CO line before line 095:

```
CO GA(1,1,1) - GA(2,1,1) = GA(5,1,1) - GA(6,1,1)
```

The chi-square from this analysis is compared with the chi-square from the step 1 analysis using the nested goodness-of-fit test. A statistically significant chi-square difference implies gender differences in path coefficients for these two groups. In the present analysis, the constrained chi-square was 64.64 ($df = 67$), and the nested chi-square difference was 0.54 ($df = 1, ns$).

The third program focuses on the gender differences in path coefficients for Republicans and Independents and includes the following CO line before line 095:

```
CO GA(3,1,1) - GA(4,1,1) = GA(5,1,1) - GA(6,1,1)
```

The chi-square from this analysis is compared with the chi-square from the step 1 analysis using the nested goodness-of-fit test. A statistically significant chi-square difference implies gender differences in path coefficients for these two groups. In the present analysis, the constrained chi-square was 79.76 ($df = 67$), and the nested chi-square difference was 15.66 ($df = 1, p < 0.01$). Using the Holm version of the Bonferroni procedure, the first and third contrasts are statistically significant, but the middle contrast is not. Thus, there is an overall interaction effect, with the gender difference in path coefficients for Democrats being statistically significantly different from the gender difference in path coefficients for Republicans and the gender difference in path coefficients for Independents being statistically significantly different from the gender difference in path coefficients for Republicans.

Effect Size of the Interaction

In addition to testing for the presence of an interaction effect, researchers often desire an index of effect size in order to gain an appreciation of the magnitude of the effect. One such index is the difference in the magnitude of the relevant latent regression coefficients. For example, in the two-group analysis for gender differences in our first example in this chapter, the path coefficient linking personableness and success was 0.95 for males and 1.88 for females, a difference of 0.93 units. Based on past experience with the measures in the study, an investigator may conclude that this is a "moderate size" difference.

A commonly used index in traditional multiple regression for interaction effect size is the incremental explained variance in the criterion that the interaction adds, over and above a "main effect" model. Such statistics are not directly available from multiple-group solutions. A statistic that provides a sense of the strength of the interaction in the sample data and that can be used in a purely descriptive (as opposed to inferential) sense is:

$$IES = [1 - (\chi^2_1/\chi^2_2)]\ 100 \qquad (2.1)$$

where IES is an "interaction effect size" index, χ^2_1 is the step 1 (unconstrained) chi-square, and χ^2_2 is the step 2 chi-square. The IES is the percentage reduction in the step 2 chi-square that results from permitting the interaction effect (via step 1). The IES for the first example in this chapter is 48.8, indicating that the step 2 chi-square is reduced by 48.8% when an interaction effect is permitted in model estimation. We fully recognize some of the anomalies that can occur with indices such as the IES that rely on ratios, and we suggest therefore that the IES be used only as a crude index of effect size for interaction analysis in multiple-indicator models.

Standardized Versus Unstandardized Coefficients

All the above examples focus on group differences in terms of unstandardized regression coefficients. Some investigators choose to conduct group comparisons on standardized regression coefficients. This practice is not recommended unless there is a strong theoretical reason for doing so. Even given such justification, the present methods of analysis usually cannot be applied because they are based on a statistical theory of covariances, not correlations (see Cudek, 1989, for elaboration). There are many statistical reasons for preferring unstandardized coefficients to standardized coefficients, and these have been noted by several methodologists (e.g., Kim & Ferree, 1981; Stone & Hollenbeck, 1989).

We illustrate one difficulty with standardized analysis here in order to provide the reader with a sense of some of the complexities. Consider the simple, traditional bivariate regression in which we regress a measure of income onto the number of years of education in order to determine the "value" of a year of education. The analysis is conducted for two different ethnic groups, African Americans and Caucasians. Suppose further that the analysis revealed identical standardized regression coefficients of 0.50 in the two groups, indicating that for every one standard deviation that education changes, income is predicted to change 0.50 standard deviation. One might conclude from these data that the "value" of education is the same in the two groups. This may not be the case. Suppose that the standard deviation for education is 3.0 in both groups but that the standard deviation for income is 15,000 for Caucasians and 6,000 for African Americans. Such a state of affairs yields unstandardized regression coefficients of 2,500 for Caucasians (indicating that for every additional year of education, income is predicted to increase by 2,500 units) but only 1,000 for African Americans (indicating that for every additional year of education, income is predicted to increase by 1,000 units). In this case, there is a clear disparity between the two groups in terms of how increased education translates into increased income.

The problem with standardized analysis is that it creates different metrics for the two groups. The metric is in units of 15,000 for Caucasians but is in units of 6,000 for African Americans. Comparing groups on these different metrics is like measuring income in units of dollars for one group but units of the British pound for another group and then comparing groups without acknowledging the difference between the dollar and the pound.[3]

Generalizability of Results Across Measures

As noted in Chapter 1, the use of multiple indicators for latent constructs is a strength because it permits estimation of regression coefficients in the context of an error theory for the observed measures. A second advantage of a multiple-indicator strategy is that it permits a formal analysis of the generalizability of interaction analyses across divergent measures. For example, suppose that a researcher was interested in the effect of stress on blood pressure and hypothesized that this effect should differ as a function of gender. In addition to a measure of blood pressure, the investigator obtained two indicators of stress for a large sample of individuals: a self-report of the number of times the individual was angry during the past week and a rating on an 11-point scale of how stressful the individual felt that the past week was for himself or herself.

One analytic strategy that the investigator might use is to conduct a traditional moderated regression analysis using only the first indicator of stress. Suppose this is done and evidence for the predicted interaction effect is observed. The researcher might then ask whether the effect generalizes across other operationalizations of stress, and therefore repeats the analysis using the second indicator of stress. If the result fails to replicate, then the investigator has less confidence in his or her conclusion.

Such generalizability analyses are important. A limitation of the traditional regression approach is that it conducts such analyses in the context of the implicit assumption that there is no random measurement error in the data. By contrast, the multiple-indicator SEM approach can be used to address such issues in the context of an error theory. Ironically, this strength of SEM has been framed in the literature as a criticism of the approach (see the exchange by Bielby, 1986a, 1986b; Henry, 1986; Sobel & Arminger, 1986; Williams & Thomson, 1986a, 1986b).

Consider the multiple-indicator model in Figure 2.2a. In this model, the weekly report of anger has been selected as the reference variable for purposes of defining the metric of the latent stress variable. The fixed value of 1.0 for the path coefficient from the latent stress variable to the observed indicator defines this relationship. Following data analysis, the value of the path coefficient from the latent stress variable to the other indicator of stress is 2.0 for males. This means that for every one unit that the latent stress variable changes (using the metric of the reference variable, adjusted for measurement error), the general rating of stress is predicted to change 2.0 units. For females, the corresponding value for this "non-fixed" measurement path coefficient turns out to be 4.0. This means that for every one unit that the latent stress variable changes (using the metric of the reference variable, adjusted for measurement error), the general rating of stress is predicted to change 4.0 units. This discrepancy in path coefficients from the latent variables to the observed indicators between males and females suggests that the two groups of individuals may be interpreting or using the general stress scale differently, raising questions about the equivalence of the measure across the two groups.

Now suppose that instead of the anger measure, the stress indicator is used as the reference variable (see Figure 2.2b). The path coefficients from the latent stress variable to the anger measure are discrepant between males and females (0.50 versus 0.25), suggesting that the anger measure is not equivalent in the two groups.

Such an analytic outcome is a signal that the results of the interaction analysis may not generalize across measures. More specifically, when corresponding non-reference

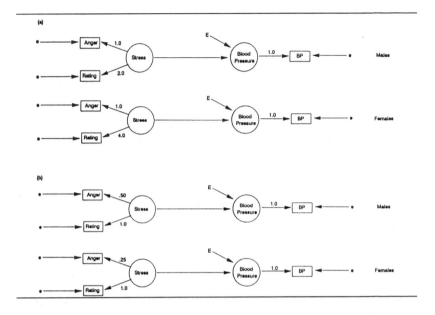

Figure 2.2. Measurement Invariance in Multiple-Group Solutions

variable path coefficients from the latent variable to the observed measures differ across groups, then the conclusions drawn with respect to an interaction analysis may change depending on which measure is chosen as the reference indicator. In our example, this is indicated by the difference between the path coefficients of 4.0 and 2.0 in Figure 2.2a. By contrast, when the values of corresponding non-reference path coefficients are equivalent across groups, the significance tests of the interaction effect will yield the same results no matter which measure is selected as the reference variable. For example, if the non-fixed path coefficient for the indicator in Figure 2.2a was equal to 2.0 for both males and females, then the test of the interaction would yield identical conclusions (but with different metrics) independent of the choice of a reference indicator.

Some methodologists (e.g., Williams & Thomson, 1986a) suggest performing a formal statistical test of group equivalence in corresponding paths of non-fixed indicators. This can be accomplished using an EQ constraint. Consider the step 1 program that was written for the first example in this chapter. This program was a multigroup solution for males and females with no constraints imposed across groups. The chi-square that resulted from this analysis was 15.25 ($df = 22$). To impose the relevant equality constraints, four EQ lines are added just before line 080:

```
EQ LX(1,2,1) LX(2,2,1)
EQ LX(1,4,2) LX(2,4,2)
```

```
EQ LY(1,2,1) LY(2,2,1)
EQ LY(1,3,1) LY(2,3,1)
```

Each line constrains a non-fixed indicator path for group 1 to equal its counterpart in group 2. The chi-square from this constrained program is then calculated (chi-square = 16.02, $df = 26$). The nested chi-square difference relative to the unconstrained step 1 program is $16.02 - 15.25 = 0.77$, $df = 4$. This difference is not statistically significant ($p > 0.05$), suggesting that a constraint that imposes identical indicator paths across groups does not significantly degrade model fit. This constrained program can then be used as the "step 1" program for formal analyses of the interaction effect of interest.

An alternative analytic strategy is to perform the traditional nested chi-square interaction analyses without the equality constraints listed above, but to repeat the analysis several times, each time changing the reference indicator. If the basic conclusion regarding the presence of the interaction effect remains unchanged across different reference indicators, then one has increased confidence in the generalizability of the conclusion. If, on the other hand, the analyses suggest that the interaction conclusions are measure dependent, then the researcher must either suspend judgment about the presence of the interaction or assert preference for a given reference indicator on theoretical or psychometric grounds and interpret the interaction accordingly.

Model Fit at Step 1

The analyses in this chapter involve the comparison of an unconstrained solution (step 1) with a constrained solution (step 2) in order to determine the adverse effects of the constraint on model fit. These analyses are predicated on the assumption that the unconstrained solution (at step 1) provides a good fit to the data. If this initial model is poor, then it makes little sense to show that adding further constraints makes the model even worse. The central issue is whether the model can be made more parsimonious by introducing equality constraints on parameters of theoretical interest, given a well-fitting unconstrained model (i.e., whether certain interaction effects can be eliminated).

In cases of multiple-group solutions, a poor fit for the unconstrained model may be the result of poor model fit in one of the groups but not the others. LISREL provides fit diagnostics for each group separately, so such scenarios can be identified. Careful examination of these diagnostics often will suggest meaningful modifications to the model that can be implemented to yield good fit to the data. If such modifications are made in one group, then they must be made in all the groups in order to use the approaches described in this monograph. A multiple-group solution assumes that the general form of the model underlying all groups is the same but that the values of the specific parameters can differ across groups, even being 0 for some groups but not others.

Main Effects and Interactions

When a moderator variable is used to define multiple groups for purposes of SEM interaction analysis, then it is not possible to examine the "main effect" of the moderator variable on the dependent variable. For example, in the first example in this chapter, we tested if the effect of personableness on judged success was different for males and females by performing a multigroup analysis in which the different groups were defined on the basis of gender. Suppose that a theorist hypothesized that gender has a direct effect on judged success, independent of this interaction. The multiple-group strategy provides no perspectives on this possibility, because gender is held constant in the analysis.

To explore such main effects, one can supplement the multiple-group analysis with an additional analysis that collapses across the various groups (i.e., that uses the total sample) and that includes gender as a predictor variable in the regression equation with the other "main effect" terms. This strategy has the disadvantage of ignoring the relevant interaction effect, which can introduce complications. Alternatively, one can explore the issue using product terms with dummy variables, but this also introduces complications (see Chapter 4 and Muthén, 1989). This two-step strategy (examining main effects and interactions separately) is not conceptually different from traditional multiple regression, in which the introduction of a product term alters the meaning of the "main effect" coefficients included in the equation, thereby rendering their interpretation away from what is traditionally meant by a main effect (see Jaccard, Turrisi, & Wan, 1990).

Tests of Equality of Covariance Matrices

When testing for group differences in parameters, some investigators adopt an approach of first conducting an overall test of the equivalence of covariance matrices between the groups (see Byrne, Shavelson, & Muthén, 1989, for a discussion of this strategy). The idea is that if differences in parameters exist between the groups, then these differences should manifest themselves as different covariance values in the groups. If the overall test fails to reject the null hypothesis of covariance equivalence, then no further analyses are conducted and the hypothesized interaction effect is declared statistically nonsignificant.

In general, we do not recommend this approach. If a theorist has a hypothesis about group differences with respect to a parameter based on substantive considerations, then it is best to adopt the strategies discussed in this chapter and move directly to the test of group differences on that parameter. The overall test of the equivalence of covariance matrices usually will have less statistical power than the more focused test (everything else being equal), making it more likely that the investigator will overlook a nonzero interaction effect.

Exploratory Group Comparisons

The methods described focus on the situation in which the interaction analyses are theoretically based and the investigator has an a priori interest in testing differences in specific parameters. It is possible to adopt an exploratory perspective in which group differences are evaluated more generally by applying equality constraints to entire matrices within the LISREL framework. For example, to test if there are group differences on *any* of the latent regression coefficients, across-group equality constraints could be applied simultaneously to the entire Gamma matrix. A statistically nonsignificant change in the chi-square as a result of such a constraint would imply that none of the coefficients in the Gamma matrix differs appreciably between the two groups. A framework for such exploratory analyses is described in Bollen (1989).

Comparison With Traditional Multiple Regression Analysis

It is instructive to briefly contrast traditional multiple regression analysis of interaction effects with a qualitative moderator variable to the analytic strategy presented in this chapter. A formal discussion of the more traditional treatment is described in Jaccard, Turrisi, and Wan (1990, p. 42). In the traditional approach, the comparison of regression coefficients for different groups of individuals uses one indicator of Y (the criterion variable), one indicator of X (the predictor variable), and one indicator of the different groups, Z (the moderator variable). The moderator variable is translated into a set of dummy variables that represent group membership, and each of these dummy variables is then multiplied by the predictor variable. Two regression analyses are then performed, one for a "main effects" model that omits the various product terms and a second for the "interaction" model that includes both "main effect" terms and the product terms. A statistically significant increase in the R^2 implies the presence of statistical interaction, and the regression coefficients associated with each product term provide information about the nature of the interaction effect.

The analysis assumes no measurement error in Y and X, an assumption that is unrealistic in many applications. The analysis also cannot accommodate the scenario in which the reliability of measures differs in the various subgroups being compared. For example, consider the case in which one of the groups consists of 7-year-olds and the second group consists of 12-year-olds. Younger children tend to provide less reliable measures than older children on a wide range of constructs. In traditional regression analysis, the reliability is assumed to be equal and perfect across all groups. If this is not true of the data, then bias in the parameter estimates can result. In contrast, the strategy advocated here uses multiple indicators of Y and X. The presence of multiple indicators permits the analytic strategy to incorporate an error theory into the parameter estimates between the variables. SEM-based analyses thus can yield more accurate and more powerful estimates of the interaction effect than traditional least squares regression analysis. SEM-based analyses explicitly take into account possible group differences in the reliability of measures. The SEM strategy uses no product terms, and the group differences are evaluated by means of nested goodness-of-fit strategies.

Another important difference between the two analytic techniques concerns the assumption of homogeneity of residuals across the various groups defined by the qualitative moderator variable. In traditional multiple regression, it is assumed that the variance of the residual scores is equal in all the groups being compared. Violations of this assumption can reduce statistical power and affect Type I errors (Alexander & DeShon, 1994). The strategies discussed in this chapter do not require the assumption of homogeneous residual variances across groups and hence are more flexible.

The SEM approach as applied to multiple indicator models typically requires the stronger statistical assumption of multivariate normality among the various Y and X measures (however, refer to the exceptions noted in Chapter 1). Issues concerning the violation of such assumptions are discussed in Chapter 5. In addition, multiple-indicator-based analyses are not as amenable to small sample analyses as traditional multiple regression models. Sample size issues are discussed in Chapter 5.

Notes

1. In this program and all future ones, each program line has a unique number. If a line is unnumbered (e.g., see the line just below line 006 with PS=SY PH=SY), then it is actually typed on the previous line. It only appears as a "separate" line because of margin restrictions in the typesetting of this book.

2. The LISREL 8 manual does not indicate that constraints of the general form $(a - b) = (c - d)$ can be used. The algebraic equivalent $a = (c - d) + b$ is permissible, however, as are other algebraically equivalent forms using a single parameter on the left side of the equation. Despite this, we found that LISREL executed constraints of the form $(a - b) = (c - d)$ and that these produced results identical to those from the other forms of the specification (e.g., $a = (c - d) + b$). For pedagogical reasons, we will use the difference approach throughout this book. In practice, however, you should double check your results against alternative specifications to ensure that there is not a problem resulting from the method of programming.

3. For multiple-group solutions, LISREL provides standardized coefficients that are characterized as "common metric completely standardized solutions." These are standardized coefficients in which a pooled covariance matrix across groups is used for purposes of standardization. We do not recommend the use of such coefficients for the types of analysis discussed in this monograph.

3. REPEATED MEASURES
AND LONGITUDINAL DESIGNS

A common scenario in the social sciences is having measures taken at multiple points in time. In these cases, a theorist might be interested in whether the value of a regression (path) coefficient changes over time. Consider the following example. A developmental psychologist hypothesizes that the extent to which a mother expresses warmth and affection to her child affects the social development of the child. The psychologist also believes that this impact is less for older children than for younger children. He or she designs a study in which mothers and children are interviewed longitudinally, once when the child is 7 years old and again when the child is 12 years old. The investigator is interested in whether the regression coefficient linking the two variables has changed over the course of the years.

The relevant path model is presented in Figure 3.1. There are three indicators of maternal warmth and affection (W1, W2, and W3) and three indicators of child social development (S1, S2, and S3). The first indicator of maternal warmth is a standard self-report measure and ranges from 0 to 10. The second indicator is based on an observer report, and the third indicator is based on reports by the spouse. Each ranges

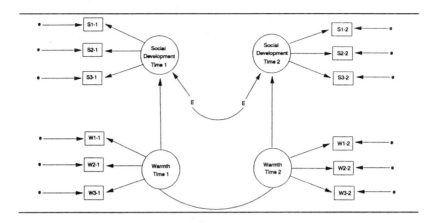

Figure 3.1. Multiple-Indicator Longitudinal Path Model

from 0 to 10. The three indicators of social development are well-known standardized tests, each ranging from 1 to 100. All measures are obtained when the child is 7 and again when the child is 12. At each time period, the latent variable of maternal warmth is assumed to influence the latent variable of social development. In addition, maternal warmth at the age of 7 is assumed to be correlated with maternal warmth at age 12. The latent residual terms reflect factors other than maternal warmth that influence social development. Because these factors are likely to be correlated over time, the residual terms are assumed to be correlated. None of the measurement residuals is assumed to be correlated with any other.

The analyses described in this chapter focus on the comparison of path/regression coefficients over time. It is also possible to use LISREL to test for *mean* changes in latent variables over time. Interested readers are referred to Jöreskog and Sorbom (1993) for a discussion of strategies that can be used for the comparison of latent variable means. The model in Figure 3.1 is programmed using the following code:

```
LINE
001    LONGITUDINAL DESIGN
002    DA NO=176 NI=12
003    LA
004    S1-1 S2-1 S3-1 W1-1 W2-1 W3-1 S1-2 S2-2 S3-2 W1-2 W2-2 W3-2
005    CM
006    80.5
007    58.6 56.5
008    53.5 44.3 49.9
009    11.4 10.2 10.0  5.9
010    10.8  8.9  8.9  3.6  4.2
011    11.3  9.0  8.9  3.7  3.1  4.4
012    18.9 14.9 14.6  3.4  5.9  4.1 59.6
```

46

```
013    15.5 12.9 13.5   2.3   4.8   3.6 41.8 45.4
014    13.7 11.7 12.4   2.4   4.5   3.0 41.7 37.4 47.3
015     9.9  7.4  7.1   2.4   2.2   2.3  7.9  6.6  5.6  5.5
016     8.1  6.5  5.9   2.2   2.1   2.2  7.1  6.3  5.6  3.4  4.3
017     6.3  5.3  4.7   1.7   1.8   1.6  5.8  5.0  4.4  3.2  2.6
3.5
018    SE
019    S1-1 S2-1 S3-1 S1-2 S2-2 S3-2 W1-1 W2-1 W3-1 W1-2 W2-2 W3-2
020    MO NX=6 NY=6 NE=2 NK=2 LX=FU LY=FU TD=SY TE=SY BE=FU GA=FU
       PS=SY PH=SY
021    LK
022    Warmth1 Warmth2
023    LE
024    Social1 Social2
025    PA LX              !          Warmth1      Warmth2
026    1 0                !   W1-1
027    1 0                !   W2-1
028    1 0                !   W3-1
029    0 1                !   W1-2
030    0 1                !   W2-2
031    0 1                !   W3-2
032    PA LY              !          Social1      Social2
033    1 0                !   S1-1
034    1 0                !   S2-1
035    1 0                !   S3-1
036    0 1                !   S1-2
037    0 1                !   S2-2
038    0 1                !   S3-2
039    PA TD              !          W1-1 W2-1 W3-1 W1-2 W2-2 W3-2
040    1                  !   W1-1
041    0 1                !   W2-1
042    0 0 1              !   W3-1
043    0 0 0 1            !   W1-2
044    0 0 0 0 1          !   W2-2
045    0 0 0 0 0 1        !   W3-2
046    PA TE              !          S1-1 S2-1 S3-1 S1-2 S2-2 S3-2
047    1                  !   S1-1
048    0 1                !   S2-1
049    0 0 1              !   S3-1
050    0 0 0 1            !   S1-2
051    0 0 0 0 1          !   S2-2
052    0 0 0 0 0 1        !   S3-2
053    PA PH              !          Warmth1      Warmth2
054    1                  !   Warmth1
055    1 1                !   Warmth2
056    PA GA              !          Warmth1      Warmth2
057    1 0                !   Social1
058    0 1                !   Social2
059    PA BE              !          Social1      Social2
060    0 0                !   Social1
```

```
061    0 0               !     Social2
062    PA PS             !              Social1     Social2
063    1                 !     Social1
064    1 1               !     Social2
065    FI LX(1,1) LX(4,2) LY(1,1) LY(4,2)    ! Set reference indicators
066    VA 1.0 LX(1,1) LX(4,2) LY(1,1) LY(4,2) ! Set reference indicators
067    OU SC RS MI
```

There are several features to note. First, because there is more than one latent Y variable, the Beta matrix is larger than a 1×1 matrix (see lines 059 to 061). Second, note that the PS matrix of variances and covariances among the latent residuals specifies the presence of correlated error, indicated by the 1 in the off-diagonal element of line 064. Third, we illustrate a new way of inputting the covariance matrix for data analysis. In this case, the covariance matrix is included directly in the program, after the CM line (see lines 006 to 017). The resulting goodness-of-fit test for the model yields a chi-square of 56.38 with 50 degrees of freedom. This is statistically nonsignificant and implies good model fit. The path going from maternal warmth to social development at age 7 is 3.09 ($p < 0.05$), and the corresponding path at age 12 is 1.82 ($p < 0.05$).

The Nested Goodness-of-Fit Test

To test formally for the equivalence of regression coefficients at ages 7 and 12, we use the nested goodness-of-fit strategy. The analysis described above is the "step 1" analysis. The step 2 analysis involves re-running the identical program, but with an equality constraint imposed for the regression coefficient at the two points in time. The equality constraint occurs just before the OU line (line 067) and appears as follows:

```
EQ GA(1,1) GA(2,2)
```

Because there is only one group in the analysis, the group parameter within the parentheses of the GA matrix on the EQ line is omitted. This line tells LISREL to generate a solution with the constraint that the coefficient in the first row and first column of the Gamma matrix must equal the coefficient in the second row and second column of the Gamma matrix. The resulting chi-square from the analysis is 66.30 with 51 degrees of freedom. The step 2 chi-square minus the step 1 chi-square is 66.30 − 56.38 = 9.92, which is distributed as a chi-square with 51 − 50 = 1 degree of freedom. This difference is statistically significant, suggesting that the two path coefficients are not equal in the population.

Interaction Analysis With More Than Two Repeated Measures

The SEM strategy is readily extended to the case of more than two time periods. Suppose that in the research example the researcher also obtained a set of measures when the children were age 17. The step 1 program would be as described previously but with the addition of the appropriate measures and latent variables. It appears as follows:

```
LINE
001    LONGITUDINAL DESIGN
002    DA NO=176 NI=18
003    LA
004    S1-1 S2-1 S3-1 W1-1 W2-1 W3-1 S1-2 S2-2 S3-2 W1-2 W2-2 W3-2
005    S1-3 S2-3 S3-3 W1-3 W2-3 W3-3
006    CM FI= LONG.DAT
007    SE
008    S1-1 S2-1 S3-1 S1-2 S2-2 S3-2 S1-3 S2-3 S3-3 W1-1 W2-1 W3-1
009    W1-2 W2-2 W3-2 W1-3 W2-3 W3-3
010    MO NX=9 NY=9 NE=3 NK=3 LX=FU LY=FU TD=SY TE=SY BE=FU GA=FU
       PS=SY PH=SY
011    LK
012    Warmth1 Warmth2 Warmth3
013    LE
014    Social1 Social2 Social3
015    PA LX              !         Warmth1      Warmth2      Warmth3
016    1 0 0              ! W1-1
017    1 0 0              ! W2-1
018    1 0 0              ! W3-1
019    0 1 0              ! W1-2
020    0 1 0              ! W2-2
021    0 1 0              ! W3-2
022    0 0 1              ! W1-3
023    0 0 1              ! W2-3
024    0 0 1              ! W3-3
025    PA LY              !         Social1      Social2      Social3
026    1 0 0              ! S1-1
027    1 0 0              ! S2-1
028    1 0 0              ! S3-1
029    0 1 0              ! S1-2
030    0 1 0              ! S2-2
031    0 1 0              ! S3-2
032    0 0 1              ! S1-3
033    0 0 1              ! S2-3
034    0 0 1              ! S3-3
035    PA TD              !         W1-1 W2-1 W3-1 W1-2 W2-2 W3-2
                                    W1-3 W2-3 W3-3
036    1                  ! W1-1
037    0 1                ! W2-1
038    0 0 1              ! W3-1
039    0 0 0 1            ! W1-2
040    0 0 0 0 1          ! W2-2
041    0 0 0 0 0 1        ! W3-2
042    0 0 0 0 0 0 1      ! W1-3
043    0 0 0 0 0 0 0 1    ! W2-3
044    0 0 0 0 0 0 0 0 1! W3-3
045    PA TE              !         S1-1 S2-1 S3-1 S1-2 S2-2 S3-2
                                    S1-3 S2-3 S3-3
```

```
046    1                    ! S1-1
047    0 1                  ! S2-1
048    0 0 1                ! S3-1
049    0 0 0 1              ! S1-2
050    0 0 0 0 1            ! S2-2
051    0 0 0 0 0 1          ! S3-2
052    0 0 0 0 0 0 1        ! S1-3
053    0 0 0 0 0 0 0 1      ! S2-3
054    0 0 0 0 0 0 0 0 1  ! S3-3
055    PA PH                !          Warmth1    Warmth2    Warmth3
056    1                    ! Warmth1
057    1 1                  ! Warmth2
058    1 1 1                ! Warmth3
059    PA GA                !          Warmth1    Warmth2    Warmth3
060    1 0 0                ! Social1
061    0 1 0                ! Social2
062    0 0 1                ! Social3
063    PA BE                !          Social1    Social2    Social3
064    0 0 0                ! Social1
065    0 0 0                ! Social2
066    0 0 0                ! Social3
067    PA PS                !          Social1    Social2    Social3
068    1                    ! Social1
069    1 1                  ! Social2
070    1 1 1                ! Social3
071    FI LX(1,1) LX(4,2) LX(7,3) LY(1,1) LY(4,2) LY(7,3)
072    VA 1.0 LX(1,1) LX(4,2) LX(7,3) LY(1,1) LY(4,2) LY(7,3)
073    OU SC RS MI
```

The input covariance matrix has been read in from a separate file in order to save space in the program (see line 006). All the pattern matrices have been adjusted to include the new measures and latent variables. The chi-square resulting from this analysis was 143.38 ($df = 126$, ns). The step 2 program is identical but adds the following line just before the OU line (line 073):

```
EQ GA(1,1) GA(2,2) GA(3,3)
```

The EQ line imposes an equality constraint on the path coefficient from parental warmth to social development at all three points in time. If the nested chi-square test yields a significant degradation in model fit, then the null hypothesis of equivalent path coefficients across the three time periods is rejected. In the present analysis, the constrained chi-square was 162.38 ($df = 128$), and the nested chi-square difference was 19.00 ($df = 2$, $p < 0.05$).

Follow-up tests then can be performed to determine which of the pairs of path coefficients are significantly different from one another. This involves performing three separate "step 2" computer runs, each with a different pairwise constraint imposed. For example, the comparison between the time 1 and time 2 path coefficients would replace the EQ line in the previous program with the following EQ line:

```
EQ GA(1,1) GA(2,2)
```

The chi-square from this model is contrasted with the chi-square from the step 1 model using the nested goodness-of-fit strategy. A statistically significant difference in the chi-squares leads to rejection of the null hypothesis that these two paths are equivalent. In the present analysis, the constrained chi-square was 152.65 ($df = 127$), and the nested chi-square difference was 9.27 ($df = 1, p < 0.05$).

The comparison between the time 1 and time 3 coefficients replaces the EQ line in the previous program with the following EQ line:

```
EQ GA(1,1) GA(3,3)
```

The chi-square from this model would be contrasted with the chi-square from the step 1 program using the nested goodness-of-fit strategy. A statistically significant difference in the chi-squares leads to rejection of the null hypothesis that these two paths are equivalent. In the present analysis, the constrained chi-square was 160.55 ($df = 127$), and the nested chi-square difference was 17.17 ($df = 1, p < 0.05$).

Finally, the comparison between the time 2 and time 3 path coefficients would replace the EQ line in the previous program with the following EQ line:

```
EQ GA(2,2) GA(3,3)
```

The chi-square from this model is contrasted with the chi-square from the step 1 program using the nested goodness-of-fit strategy. In the present analysis, the constrained chi-square was 144.26 ($df = 127$), and the nested chi-square difference was 0.88 ($df = 1$, ns). A modified Bonferroni control for experimentwise error can be imposed across the set of contrasts, if it is theoretically appropriate to do so.

Three-Way Interactions

It is possible to combine the analytic strategy in this chapter with the analytic strategy in Chapter 2 to examine three-way interaction effects. For example, suppose we suspected that the path differences in the effects of parental warmth on social development over time are more magnified for girls than for boys. To test this, we first perform a "step 1" analysis using stacked programs in which all paths are free to vary within the two gender groups and no equality constraints are imposed. The program code is as follows:

```
LINE
001    MALES - THREE WAY INTERACTION
002    DA NG=2 NO=87 NI=12
003    LA
004    S1-1 S2-1 S3-1 W1-1 W2-1 W3-1 S1-2 S2-2 S3-2 W1-2 W2-2 W3-2
```

```
005    CM FI= LOMALE.DAT
006    SE
007    S1-1 S2-1 S3-1 S1-2 S2-2 S3-2 W1-1 W2-1 W3-1 W1-2 W2-2 W3-2
008    MO NX=6 NY=6 NE=2 NK=2 LX=FU LY=FU TD=SY TE=SY BE=FU GA=FU
       PS=SY PH=SY
009    LK
010    Warmth1 Warmth2
011    LE
012    Social1 Social2
013    PA LX          !           Warmth1     Warmth2
014    1 0            ! W1-1
015    1 0            ! W2-1
016    1 0            ! W3-1
017    0 1            ! W1-2
018    0 1            ! W2-2
019    0 1            ! W3-2
020    PA LY          !           Social1      Social2
021    1 0            ! S1-1
022    1 0            ! S2-1
023    1 0            ! S3-1
024    0 1            ! S1-2
025    0 1            ! S2-2
026    0 1            ! S3-2
027    PA TD          !           W1-1 W2-1 W3-1 W1-2 W2-2 W3-2
028    1              ! W1-1
029    0 1            ! W2-1
030    0 0 1          ! W3-1
031    0 0 0 1        ! W1-2
032    0 0 0 0 1      ! W2-2
033    0 0 0 0 0 1    ! W3-2
034    PA TE          !           S1-1 S2-1 S3-1 S1-2 S2-2 S3-2
035    1              ! S1-1
036    0 1            ! S2-1
037    0 0 1          ! S3-1
038    0 0 0 1        ! S1-2
039    0 0 0 0 1      ! S2-2
040    0 0 0 0 0 1    ! S3-2
041    PA PH          !           Warmth1     Warmth2
042    1              ! Warmth1
043    1 1            ! Warmth2
044    PA GA          !           Warmth1     Warmth2
045    1 0            ! Social1
046    0 1            ! Social2
047    PA BE          !           Social1     Social2
048    0 0            ! Social1
049    0 0            ! Social2
050    PA PS          !           Social1     Social2
051    1              ! Social1
052    1 1            ! Social2
```

```
053    FI LX(1,1) LX(4,2) LY(1,1) LY(4,2)    ! Set reference indicators
054    VA 1.0 LX(1,1) LX(4,2) LY(1,1) LY(4,2) ! Set reference indicators
055    OU SC RS MI
056    FEMALES - THREE WAY INTERACTION
057    DA NO=89 NI=12
058    LA
059    S1-1 S2-1 S3-1 W1-1 W2-1 W3-1 S1-2 S2-2 S3-2 W1-2 W2-2 W3-2
060    CM FI= LOFEM.DAT
061    SE
062    S1-1 S2-1 S3-1 S1-2 S2-2 S3-2 W1-1 W2-1 W3-1 W1-2 W2-2 W3-2
063    MO NX=6 NY=6 NE=2 NK=2 LX=PS LY=PS TD=PS TE=PS BE=PS GA=PS
       PS=PS PH=PS
064    LK
065    Warmth1 Warmth2
066    LE
067    Social1 Social2
068    OU SC RS MI
```

The chi-square test of fit for this analysis was 93.43 ($df = 100$). The "step 2" program adds a constraint line before the OU line of group 2 (line 068) that has the following form:

```
CO GA(1,1,1) - GA(1,2,2) = GA(2,1,1) - GA(2,2,2)
```

This constraint forces LISREL to estimate parameters under the restriction that the difference in path coefficients for males must equal the difference in path coefficients for females. If this constraint adversely affects model fit relative to the "step 1" analysis, then a three-way interaction is present (barring a Type I error). In the present analysis, the constrained chi-square was 111.28 ($df = 101$), and the nested chi-square difference was 17.85 ($df = 1$, $p < 0.01$). A three-way interaction is evident.

Three-Way Interactions With More Than Two Groups

The analytic strategy is readily extended to the case of multiple time periods and multiple groups, using the logic described in Chapter 2 for three-way interactions involving more than two groups. When there are more than two time periods, then the procedures discussed in earlier sections of this chapter are applied across the multiple groups.

Effect Size of the Interaction

Indices of the effect size of the interaction can be obtained using procedures similar to those described in the previous chapter. One index is simply the difference in the magnitude of the path coefficients in question. For example, in the first example in this chapter, the path coefficient linking parental warmth and social development was 3.09 for 7-year-olds and 1.82 for 12-year-olds, a difference of 1.27 units. Based on past experience with the measures, an investigator may conclude that this is a "small" difference. The IES for the first example in this chapter is 15.0, indicating that the step 2 chi-square is reduced by 15.0% when an interaction effect is estimated.

Generalizability of Results Across Measures

The issues discussed in the previous chapter with respect to generalizability of results across measures hold with equal vigor for repeated measure analysis of interactions. Analytic strategies that impose equality constraints across corresponding non-fixed indicator measures over time can be used to evaluate formally the generalizability of results across measures.

Comparison With Traditional Multiple Regression Analysis

There are few discussions in the literature on the analysis of differences in regression coefficients as a function of repeated measures or longitudinal designs. Cohen and Cohen (1983) provide details for such analyses that require dummy variables for each respondent in the study. The analytic method is problematic in terms of computer memory when the number of respondents is large. Cohen and Cohen (1983) also describe methods for circumventing these practical limitations. Both approaches described by Cohen and Cohen rely on a product term approach. Although straightforward, the methods are somewhat tedious to apply, especially for more complex designs. As before, the analyses rely on single indicators of each variable and assume that all measures are perfectly reliable. The presence of unreliability introduces bias into the parameter estimates and reduces statistical power for the analysis of statistical interaction. In addition, multiple regression methods cannot easily accommodate complex error theories that involve correlated and systematic error.

The multiple-indicator based strategy does not rely on product terms and does not require the use of dummy variables for individual respondents. Because of the presence of multiple indicators, the analysis can be undertaken in the context of an error theory. The error theory can be complex, including correlated errors, systematic errors, and random errors (unreliability). For more complex analyses involving three-way interactions with multiple groups of individuals, SEM analyses can take into account group differences in the error structure underlying the data.

4. THE USE OF PRODUCT TERMS

When all three variables (criterion, predictor, and moderator) are continuous, then an effective means for the analysis of (bilinear) statistical interaction uses product terms. To illustrate the approach, we use the example from Chapter 1, in which the quality of the parent-teen relationship was hypothesized to moderate the impact of peer pressure on drug use. There are three latent variables (peer pressure, relationship quality, and drug use), each with three indicators. One strategy for testing the interaction is to form all possible product terms between the various peer pressure and relationship quality indicators and then use these product terms as indicators of a latent product variable (see Figure 1.3). The different parameters are then estimated using the standard LISREL programming strategy.

Such an approach would yield erroneous results. The problem is that the measurement error (i.e., the e score) for a given product indicator must be a function of the measurement error of the component parts of the product term. For example, the error variance for the indicator P1Q2 is a function of the error variance for P1 and the error variance for Q2, as well as other aspects of the underlying model. Any estimates of the measurement error for P1Q2 must respect these mathematical relations. Unless LISREL somehow is made aware of these constraints, as well as others that result from the use of product terms, it will estimate parameters without regard for the mathematical intricacies involved. LISREL 8 permits the programming of such constraints.

Additional Matrices in LISREL

There have been several approaches to using product terms with latent variables, each of which relies on the pioneering work of Kenny and Judd (1984; see Jaccard & Wan, 1995a; Jöreskog & Yang, 1996; Ping, 1994, 1995, 1996). We present the approach of Jöreskog and Yang (1996). In developing the analytic strategy, we assume that the reader is familiar with the material in Appendix A.

The programming strategy requires four new matrices in LISREL, the Kappa matrix, the Alpha matrix, the Tau-X matrix, and the Tau-Y matrix. The Kappa matrix (abbreviated KA) focuses on the latent variable means for the predictor variables. If there are three latent predictor variables, then Kappa has three elements. For example, the following programming lines

```
PA KA
1 1 1
```

instruct LISREL to estimate the means of the three latent predictor variables (where each 1 refers to a different latent variable, in the order that they appear on the LK line). The Alpha matrix focuses on the intercept in the regression equation of the latent variables. Let F_Y, F_X, and F_Z represent the latent Y, X, and Z variables, respectively. The (product term) regression equation for these latent variables is

$$F_Y = \alpha + \beta_1 F_X + \beta_2 F_Z + \beta_3 F_X F_Z + \varepsilon \tag{4.1}$$

where α is the intercept, β_i is a regression coefficient, and ε is the residual. The programming lines

```
PA AL
1
```

instruct LISREL to estimate α.

The Tau-X matrix focuses on a different regression equation, namely the equation that regresses an observed predictor indicator variable onto its underlying latent variable. For example, in Figure 1.3, the regression of the observed variable P1 onto its corresponding latent variable of peer pressure, F_X, yields the following equation:

$$P1 = \tau_{P1} + \gamma_{P1}F_X + \delta_{P1} \tag{4.2}$$

where τ_{P1} is an intercept term, γ_{P1} is a regression coefficient (that corresponds to an element in the LX matrix), and δ_{P1} is a residual (that corresponds to an element in the TD matrix). In Figure 1.3, there are 15 observed X variables (P1, P2, P3, Q1, Q2, Q3, P1Q1, P1Q2, . . . , P3Q3), and each has a regression equation corresponding to Equation 4.2. The programming lines

```
PA TX
1 1 1 1 1 1 1 1 1 1 1 1 1 1 1
```

instruct LISREL to estimate the intercept term τ_{Xi} for each of the 15 regression equations representing the predictor indicators (in the order listed on the LA line, unless they are reordered using the SE line).

Finally, the Tau-Y matrix has the same function as the Tau-X matrix, but for the observed Y indicator variables regressed onto their underlying latent variable. The programming lines

```
PA TY
1 1 1
```

instruct LISREL to estimate the intercept terms τ_{Yi} for each of the (three) regression equations representing a criterion indicator (see Figure 1.3).

In practice, it usually is not possible to estimate all the parameters specified in KA, AL, TX, and TY in conjunction with the other matrices from previous chapters, because to do so would yield an underidentified model. Furthermore, the parameters from KA, AL, TX, and TY were not necessary for our prior applications. For product term analysis, however, the parameters can be taken into account to yield appropriate statistical constraints via the Jöreskog and Yang (1996) method.

Statistical Constraints for Product Term Analysis

For the model in Figure 1.3, there are three indicators of F_X (peer pressure) and three indicators of F_Z (relationship quality). These can be used to form nine possible product indicators, P1Q1, P1Q2, . . . , P3Q3. Jöreskog and Yang (1996) argue that it is not necessary to use all nine indicators of the product term to test for statistical interaction. In fact, they suggest that it is possible to obtain good results using only a single indicator of the product term, P1Q1, based on the two variables that serve as the reference indicators for F_X and F_Z. We adopt this approach here because it simplifies programming considerably and minimizes the number of input variables that are characterized by non-normal distributions (see the discussion below that elaborates on this advantage). For situations in which more product indicators are desired, readers are referred to Jöreskog and Yang (1996).

The programming strategy that we use is slightly different from the one described by Jöreskog and Yang. Their strategy is more efficient, but it is not easily understood in the context of the programming approach from previous chapters. Our strategy yields results identical to those of the programs developed by Jöreskog and Yang (1996). The statistical constraints that must be imposed are the following (see Jöreskog & Yang, 1996, for the mathematical derivation of these constraints):

Constraint 1: The mean values for F_X and F_Z must be "fixed" to be 0. This constraint forces the latent X and Z variables to be "mean centered" (i.e., in deviation score form). This constraint is imposed with reference to the KA matrix.

Constraint 2: The mean of the product latent variable, $F_X F_Z$, must equal the covariance between F_X and F_Z. This constraint involves the Kappa and Phi matrices.

Constraint 3: The covariance of F_X and $F_X F_Z$ must be "fixed" to equal 0, and the covariance of F_Z and $F_X F_Z$ must also be "fixed" to equal 0. This constraint is imposed with reference to the Phi matrix. This constraint derives from the fact that the latent variables are in deviation score form and, given multivariate normality, the component parts of the product term will be uncorrelated with the product term.

Constraint 4: The variance of $F_X F_Z$ must equal the variance of F_X times the variance of F_Z plus the squared covariance of F_X with F_Z. This constraint is imposed with reference to the Phi matrix and follows from derivations by Anderson (1984).

Constraint 5: Coefficient α must be constrained to equal 0. This constraint is necessary for the model to be identified. The imposition of the constraint assists us in estimating the regression coefficients in Equation 4.1, but it also renders the interpretation of the elements of Tau-Y ambiguous (which generally are not of substantive interest). See Jöreskog and Yang (1996) for details.

Constraint 6: The variance of the measurement residual (δ_{X1Z1}) for the observed product term, X1Z1, must satisfy the following equation:

$$\text{var}(\delta_{X1Z1}) = \tau_{X1}{}^2 \text{var}(\delta_{Z1}) + \tau_{Z1}{}^2 \text{var}(\delta_{X1}) + \text{var}(F_X)\text{var}(\delta_{Z1}) \qquad (4.3)$$
$$+ \text{var}(F_Z)\text{var}(\delta_{X1}) + \text{var}(\delta_{X1})\text{var}(\delta_{Z1})$$

where τ_{X1} is the intercept based on Equation 4.2 for the reference indicator (X1) regressed onto F_X, τ_{Z1} is the intercept based on Equation 4.2 for the reference indicator (Z1) regressed onto F_Z, $\text{var}(\delta_{X1})$ is the residual variance for X1, var(δ_{Z1}) is the residual variance for Z1, var(F_X) is the variance of F_X, and var(F_Z) is the variance of F_Z. These constraints are imposed with reference to the Tau-X matrix, the Phi matrix, and the Theta Delta matrix.

Constraint 7: The covariance between δ_{X1} and δ_{X1Z1} must equal τ_{Z1}var(δ_{X1}), and the covariance between δ_{Z1} and δ_{X1Z1} must equal τ_{X1}var(δ_{Z1}). These constraints are imposed with reference to the Tau-X matrices and the Theta Delta matrix.

Constraint 8: The intercept for the regression of X1Z1 onto F_XF_Z (see Equation 4.2) must equal the intercept for X1 times the intercept for Z1; that is, it must equal $(\tau_{X1})(\tau_{Z1})$. This constraint is implemented with reference to the Tau-X matrix.

Constraint 9: The observed product term, X1Z1, is influenced by F_X and F_Z. The path from F_X to X1Z1 must equal τ_{Z1}, and the path from F_Z to X1Z1 must equal τ_{X1}. X1Z1 is then used to define the metric of the latent product variable F_XF_Z by fixing the path from F_XF_Z to X1Z1 to equal 1.

Estimation Issues

Estimation of parameters within LISREL typically is accomplished using a maximum likelihood criterion in which multivariate normality among the variables is assumed. The presence of a product term violates this assumption, even when there is no statistical interaction. This is because the products of normally distributed variables are not themselves distributed normally. This nonnormality can undermine the statistical analysis. Monte Carlo studies in other contexts suggest that maximum likelihood analysis is robust to certain violations of the multivariate normality assumption (e.g., Bollen, 1989) and, hence, this may not be problematic.

An alternative to the traditional maximum likelihood method is to use a weighted least squares (WLS) solution. This approach is "distribution free" and does not require the restrictive assumption of multivariate normality. Studies have shown, however, that effective use of the approach requires large sample sizes that may be unrealistic in most social science research (e.g., Jöreskog & Sorbom, 1993). Jöreskog and Yang (1996) note certain technical problems with the traditional WLS solution for product terms and discuss possible remedies. Implementation of the appropriate WLS solution requires novel programming coupled with extremely large sample sizes. Preliminary evidence suggests that a maximum likelihood approach with product terms will perform satisfactorily for moderate sample sizes in conditions that characterize many social science applications (see Jaccard & Wan, 1995a; Ping, 1994, 1995, 1996). The approach tends to yield unbiased parameter estimates of the regression coefficients and, when used in a traditional hypothesis testing paradigm, yields Type I error rates for regression coefficients that are close to the theoretically specified alpha (of 0.05).

We applied the Jöreskog and Yang method using maximum likelihood with a single product indicator to several of the simulation conditions reported by Jaccard and Wan (1995a) and found no evidence for inflated Type I errors for the latent variable regression coefficients. In addition, we observed unbiased parameter estimates and a reasonably well-behaved overall chi-square test. Generally speaking, we believe that a maximum likelihood analysis will yield satisfactory results for simple regression models. The standard errors for parameter estimates should be viewed as "guidelines" rather than "correct" standard errors but probably will perform satisfactorily for simple hypothesis testing frameworks that test the "statistical significance" of regression coefficients against a null hypothesis of 0. Technically, the overall chi-square test of model fit is incorrect. Alternative fit indices that do not rely on the sampling distribution of the chi-square therefore should be scrutinized when evaluating model fit (e.g., the CFI and the standardized root mean square residual).

Programming Strategies

To illustrate LISREL programming, we focus on the drug use example from Chapter 1 (Figure 1.3), but with only a single product term indicator. To simplify, we program a model that omits the correlated error in the observed drug use residuals. The three indicators of drug use all range from 0 to 10, with higher scores indicating increased drug use. The first indicator of peer pressure used a semantic differential scale ranging from −3 to +3, with higher numbers indicating greater perceived peer pressure. The remaining indicators each range from 1 to 10, with higher scores indicating greater perceived pressure to use drugs. The three indicators for quality of the relationship with the parent ranged from −3 to +3, with higher scores indicating higher quality. Here is the program code with the above constraints imposed:

```
LINE
001    TEST OF PRODUCT TERM MODEL
002    DA NI=10 NO=800
003    LA
004    D1 D2 D3 P1 P2 P3 Q1 Q2 Q3 P1Q1
005    ME FI = MEAN.DAT
006    CM FI = COV.DAT
007    MO NY=3 NE=1 NK=3 NX=7 LX=FU LY=FU TD=SY TE=SY PH=SY PS=SY C
008    GA=FU BE=FU KA=FU TX=FU TY=FU AL=FU
009    LK
010    Peer Quality Product
011    LE
012    DrugUse
013    PA LY            !         DrugUse
014    1               ! D1
015    1               ! D2
016    1               ! D3
017    PA LX            !         Peer      Quality      Product
018    1 0 0           ! P1
019    1 0 0           ! P2
020    1 0 0           ! P3
021    0 1 0           ! Q1
```

```
022    0 1 0                   ! Q2
023    0 1 0                   ! Q3
024    1 1 1                   ! P1Q1  (See constraint 9)
025    PA TE                   !        D1  D2  D3
026    1                       ! D1
027    0 1                     ! D2
028    0 0 1                   ! D3
029    PA GA                   !          Peer        Quality      Product
030    1 1 1                   ! DrugUse
031    PA BE                   !          DrugUse
032    0                       ! DrugUse
033    PA PS                   !          DrugUse
034    1                       ! DrugUse
035    PA KA                   !          Peer        Quality      Product
036    0 0 1                   ! Mean Values (see Constraint 1)
037    CO KA(3)=PH(2,1)        ! See Constraint 2
038    PA PH                   !          Peer        Quality      Product
039    1                       ! Peer
040    1 1                     ! Quality
041    0 0 1                   ! Product (see Constraint 3)
042    CO PH(3,3)=PH(1,1)*PH(2,2)+PH(2,1)*PH(2,1)   ! See Constraint 4
043    PA AL                   ! Intercept for product term equation
044    0                       ! See constraint 5
045    PA TD                   !          P1  P2  P3  Q1  Q2  Q3  P1Q1
046    1                       ! P1
047    0 1                     ! P2
048    0 0 1                   ! P3
049    0 0 0 1                 ! Q1
050    0 0 0 0 1               ! Q2
051    0 0 0 0 0 1             ! Q3
052    1 0 0 1 0 0 1           ! P1Q1 (See Constraints 6 and 7)
053    CO TD(7,7)=TX(1)*TX(1)*TD(4,4) + TX(4)*TX(4)*TD(1,1)
       + PH(1,1)*TD(4,4) +
054    PH(2,2)*TD(1,1) + TD(1,1)*TD(4,4)   ! See Constraint 6
055    CO TD(7,1)=TX(4)*TD(1,1)            ! See Constraint 7
056    CO TD(7,4)=TX(1)*TD(4,4)            ! See Constraint 7
057    PA TY
058    1 1 1
059    PA TX
060    1 1 1 1 1 1 1
061    CO TX(7)=TX(1)*TX(4)                ! See Constraint 8
062    CO LX(7,1) = TX(4)                  ! See Constraint 9
063    CO LX(7,2) = TX(1)                  ! See Constraint 9
064    FI LX(1,1) LX(4,2) LX(7,3) LY(1,1)  ! Set reference indicators
065    VA 1.0 LX(1,1) LX(4,2) LX(7,3) LY(1,1) ! Set reference indicators
066    OU SC RS MI AD=OFF IT=200
```

Line 005 inputs the means of the sample data, in the order specified on the LA line (see lines 003 and 004). The means are necessary to estimate the various intercept terms.

They are in a file called "MEAN.DAT" and are in free format (i.e., separated by a comma or a blank). Line 007 is the MO line, which ends with a "C." A "C" means that the line is too long and is continued on the next line. This was also necessary on line 053 for Constraint 6. Line 024 establishes the foundation for Constraint 9 by indicating that the paths from F_X to X1Z1 and from F_Z to X1Z1 are to be estimated, then further denotes the path from F_XF_Z to X1Z1, which is later fixed to 1.0 in lines 064 and 065 to serve as a reference variable. Line 036 imposes Constraint 1 by setting all latent predictor means to 0, except for the latent product term. Line 037 imposes Constraint 2 by forcing the mean of the latent product variable to equal the covariance between F_X and F_Z. Line 041 imposes Constraint 3 by fixing the covariance between F_X and F_XF_Z to 0 and F_Z and F_XF_Z to 0. Line 042 imposes Constraint 4, and line 044 fixes the latent intercept at 0 (Constraint 5). Line 052 indicates that there will be correlated error for X1 and X1Z1 and for Z1 and X1Z1, and that these must be estimated (as dictated by Constraint 7). The remaining CO lines follow directly from Constraints 6 through 9. The OU line (line 066) has two new parameters. AD=OFF turns off LISREL's internal admissibility check. IT=200 sets the upper limit for the number of iterations that LISREL performs to 200. We have found that these parameters are necessary in order to converge to an adequate solution in some cases.

For the present data, the overall fit of the model was good. The RMSEA was 0.034, the standardized RMR was 0.019, the GFI was 0.98, the CFI was 0.99, and all other indices point to a satisfactory model. Table 4.1 presents abbreviated output. From the section LISREL ESTIMATES and the subsection SQUARED MULTIPLE CORRELATIONS FOR STRUCTURAL EQUATIONS, the estimated latent variable squared multiple correlation of 0.48 is found, indicating that the latent predictors accounted for 48% of the variance in latent drug use. The sections for the SQUARED MULTIPLE CORRELATIONS FOR Y - VARIABLES and SQUARED MULTIPLE CORRELATIONS FOR X - VARIABLES provide the reliability estimates for the observed measures (including the product indicator). The GAMMA matrix from the output contains the regression coefficients of interest. They are $b_1 = 1.14$ for the latent peer pressure, $b_2 = -.48$ for the latent quality of the parent-teen relationship, and $b_3 = -0.99$ for the latent product term. The coefficient for the latent product term is statistically significant ($z = -13.15$, $p < 0.05$), suggesting the presence of an interaction effect. For every one unit that the quality of the parent-teen relationship increases, the impact of peer pressure on drug use decreases by 0.99 units.

The regression coefficients can be manipulated using the procedures described in Jaccard, Turrisi, and Wan (1990) to gain an appreciation for the slope of drug use on peer pressure at different values of relationship quality. Specifically, the slope, b, at a given value of Z is

$$b \text{ at } V_Z = b_1 + b_3 V_Z \qquad (4.4)$$

where V_Z is a specific value of Z. Because the latent variables are mean centered, a score of 0 on Z corresponds to the mean of Z. Substituting the value of 0 for V_Z and using the values of 1.14 and $-.99$ for b_1 and b_3 in Equation 4.4, respectively, yields a

TABLE 4.1
Abbreviated LISREL Output for Product Term Analysis

LISREL ESTIMATES (MAXIMUM LIKELIHOOD)

SQUARED MULTIPLE CORRELATIONS FOR STRUCTURAL EQUATIONS

DrugUse

0.48

SQUARED MULTIPLE CORRELATIONS FOR Y - VARIABLES

D1	D2	D3
0.88	0.84	0.83

SQUARED MULTIPLE CORRELATIONS FOR X - VARIABLES

P1	P2	P3	Q1	Q2	Q3	P1Q1
0.81	0.70	0.69	0.89	0.81	0.77	0.76

GAMMA

	Pressure	Quality	Product
DrugUse	1.14	-.48	-0.99
	(0.08)	(0.06)	(0.08)
	15.15	-8.22	-13.15

PHI

	Pressure	Quality	Product
Pressure	0.47		
Quality	0.26	0.68	
Product	—	—	0.38

---

slope of 1.14. When the quality of the parent-teen relationship latent variable is at its mean, the impact of peer pressure on drug use is estimated to be 1.14. For every one unit that peer pressure increases (using the metric of the peer reference indicator, P1), drug use is predicted to increase by 1.14 units (using the metric of the drug use reference indicator, D1).

From the PHI Matrix under LISREL ESTIMATES, the variance of the latent quality variable is 0.68, and the square root of this is the estimated latent variable standard deviation (0.82). The effect of peer pressure on drug use when the latent quality score is "low" (i.e., one estimated standard deviation below its mean) is found by substituting the value of –0.82 for V_Z in Equation 4.4 and using the values of 1.14 and –.99 for b_1 and b_3, respectively. The result is 1.95. When the quality of the parent-teen relationship is poor (as reflected by a value that is one estimated standard deviation below its mean), a one unit increase in peer pressure yields a predicted 1.95 unit increase in drug use.

The effect of peer pressure on drug use when the latent quality score is "high" (i.e., one estimated standard deviation above its mean) is found by substituting the value of +0.82 for V_Z in Equation 4.4 with the appropriate values of b_1 and b_3. The result is 0.33. When the quality of the parent-teen relationship is good (as reflected by a value that is one estimated standard deviation above its mean), a one unit increase in peer pressure yields a predicted 0.33 unit increase in drug use.

Some comments about the interpretation of b_1 and b_2 should be made. These values do *not* represent "main effects" in the traditional sense of this term, but rather conditional effects of one variable when the other variable is at its mean. Usually, the values of these coefficients will be close to the corresponding coefficients that would result from a "main effects" only analysis, although it is possible for discrepancies to occur. They will exactly equal the values of a "main effect" only model if the latent "main effect" variables are multivariately normally distributed, an assumption that we make for our product term analyses.

Three-Way Interactions

It is possible to combine the analytic strategy used in this chapter with the analytic strategy in Chapter 2 to examine three-way interaction effects. For example, suppose we suspected that the moderating influence of the quality of the parent-teen relationship was stronger for females than for males. This three-way interaction predicts that the path coefficient for the latent product term differs as a function of gender. We first perform a "step 1" analysis using stacked programs in which all paths are free to vary within the two groups. The program code is as follows:

```
LINE
001    MALES - TEST OF THREE WAY INTERACTION
002    DA NG=2 NI=10 NO=240
003    LA
004    D1 D2 D3 P1 P2 P3 Q1 Q2 Q3 P1Q1
005    ME FI = MEAN.DAT
006    CM FI = COV.DAT
007    MO NY=3 NE=1 NK=3 NX=7 LX=FU LY=FU TD=SY TE=SY PH=SY PS=SY C
008    GA=FU BE=FU KA=FU TX=FU TY=FU AL=FU
009    LK
010    Peer Quality Product
011    LE
012    DrugUse
013    PA LY              !  DrugUse
014    1                  !  D1
015    1                  !  D2
```

```
016   1                     ! D3
017   PA LX                 !            Peer      Quality    Product
018   1 0 0                 ! P1
019   1 0 0                 ! P2
020   1 0 0                 ! P3
021   0 1 0                 ! Q1
022   0 1 0                 ! Q2
023   0 1 0                 ! Q3
024   1 1 1                 ! P1Q1 (See constraint 9)
025   PA TE                 !      D1  D2  D3
026   1                     ! D1
027   0 1                   ! D2
028   0 0 1                 ! D3
029   PA GA                 !            Peer      Quality    Product
030   1 1 1                 ! DrugUse
031   PA BE                 !            DrugUse
032   0                     ! DrugUse
033   PA PS                 !            DrugUse
034   1                     ! DrugUse
035   PA KA                 !            Peer      Quality    Product
036   0 0 1                 ! Mean Values (see Constraint 1)
037   CO KA(3)=PH(2,1) ! See Constraint 2
038   PA PH                 !            Peer      Quality    Product
039   1                     ! Peer
040   1 1                   ! Quality
041   0 0 1                 ! Product (see Constraint 3)
042   CO PH(3,3)=PH(1,1)*PH(2,2)+PH(2,1)*PH(2,1)  ! See Constraint 4
043   PA AL                 ! Intercept for product term equation
044   0                     ! See constraint 5
045   PA TD                 !            P1  P2  P3  Q1  Q2  Q3  P1Q1
046   1                     ! P1
047   0 1                   ! P2
048   0 0 1                 ! P3
049   0 0 0 1               ! Q1
050   0 0 0 0 1             ! Q2
051   0 0 0 0 0 1           ! Q3
052   1 0 0 1 0 0 1         ! P1Q1 (See Constraints 6 and 7)
053   CO TD(7,7)=TX(1)*TX(1)*TD(4,4) + TX(4)*TX(4)*TD(1,1)
      + PH(1,1)*TD(4,4) + C
054   PH(2,2)*TD(1,1) + TD(1,1)*TD(4,4)  ! See Constraint 6
055   CO TD(7,1)=TX(4)*TD(1,1)            ! See Constraint 7
056   CO TD(7,4)=TX(1)*TD(4,4)            ! See Constraint 7
057   PA TY
058   1 1 1
059   PA TX
060   1 1 1 1 1 1 1
061   CO TX(7)=TX(1)*TX(4)                ! See Constraint 8
062   CO LX(7,1) = TX(4)                  ! See Constraint 9
063   CO LX(7,2) = TX(1)                  ! See Constraint 9
064   FI LX(1,1) LX(4,2) LX(7,3) LY(1,1)  ! Set reference indicators
```

```
065    VA 1.0 LX(1,1) LX(4,2) LX(7,3) LY(1,1) ! Set reference indicators
066    OU SC RS MI AD=OFF IT=200
067    FEMALES - TEST OF THREE WAY INTERACTION
068    DA NI=10 NO=303
069    LA
070    D1 D2 D3 P1 P2 P3 Q1 Q2 Q3 P1Q1
071    ME FI = FEMMEAN.DAT
072    CM FI = FEMCOV.DAT
073    MO NX=7 NY=3 NE=1 NK=3 LX=PS LY=PS TD=PS TE=PS PH=PS BE=PS
       GA=PS PS=PS C
074    KA=PS AL=PS TX=PS TY=PS
075    LK
076    Pressure Quality Product
077    LE
078    DrugUse
079    OU SC MI RS AD=OFF IT=200
```

The "step 2" program is then executed with an equality constraint added just before the output line for the last group (line 079). This equality constraint forces the path coefficient for the latent product variable to be equal in the two groups. The constraint appears as follows:

```
EQ GA(1,1,3) GA(2,1,3)
```

If the difference in goodness-of-fit tests between the "step 1" and "step 2" analyses is substantial and of practical significance, then a three-way interaction exists. If the difference is not significant, then we fail to reject the hypothesis of a three-way interaction.

Effect Size of the Interaction

Indices of the effect size of the interaction can be obtained in several ways. One index is simply the value of the coefficient associated with the latent product term. For example, in the analysis in our first example in this chapter, the path coefficient for the latent product term was −0.96. Based on past experience with the measures in the study, an investigator may conclude that this represents a "small" change in slopes given a one unit change in the moderator variable. A second (somewhat crude) index is the proportion of explained variance in the latent criterion variable that the interaction effect accounts for in the sample data. This effect size index is calculated by subtracting from the relevant standardized psi coefficient for the product term program the corresponding psi coefficient in a program that omits the interaction.

Generalizability of Results Across Measures

The issues discussed in previous chapters with respect to generalizability of results across measures hold with equal vigor for product term analyses. The robustness of results when different reference indicators are used for the latent variables should be explored. For analyses of three-way interactions using multiple-group solutions, analytic strategies that impose equality constraints across corresponding non-fixed indicator measures can be used effectively, as discussed in previous chapters.

Centering

Kenny and Judd (1984) recommend that raw scores be mean centered prior to the formation of product terms and formal analysis. The approaches and constraints of Ping (1994, 1995) and Jaccard and Wan (1995a) assume such mean centering. Given multivariate normality, centering reduces the correlation between X1 and the product term X1Z1 (and between Z1 and X1Z1) to 0. This can be desirable when high levels of collinearity between these terms interfere with the computational algorithms of regression programs.

The programming strategy in this chapter does not require centering of raw scores and thus is more flexible than the other approaches. It takes into account the mathematical relations between the various intercept terms and other parameter estimates so that centering is not required. In fact, Jöreskog and Yang (1996) describe situations in which centering can be problematic for product term analyses with latent variables when a WLS solution is pursued. For the maximum likelihood approach described in this chapter, we have observed instances in which LISREL was able to converge effectively on a solution only when the variables composing the product term were first centered prior to the formation of the product term. This probably will be necessary if X1 is highly correlated with X1Z1 and Z1 is highly correlated with X1Z1, to the point that it interferes with LISREL's algorithm for parameter estimation. The program strategy described in this chapter can be applied to the centered data with minimal negative practical impact. Of course, centering of the latent F_X and F_Z variables (as described in Constraint 1) is essential to the programming strategy.

Multiple Product Terms

There are occasions when an analyst will focus on two or more latent product terms in the same equation and when a given latent variable is present in both product terms. For example, in addition to the latent product term between peer approval of drug use and relationship quality, a latent product term might also be included between the latent variable of peer approval of drug use and a latent variable of social class (under the hypothesis that peer influence is greater for lower-class individuals).

Suppose social class has two indicators, SC1 and SC2. The product indicator for the first latent product term is P1 times Q1, and for the second product term it is P1 times SC1. Programming follows all the conventions noted above for the two sets of product terms, separately. The presence of P1 in both sets of product terms, however, means that there will be correlated errors in measurement residuals of the product terms (in the TD matrix) across the two sets. The relevant constraints that must be imposed can be derived based on the discussion by Jöreskog and Yang (1996).

Complex Interactions With Continuous Variables

The product term analyses described thus far focus on interaction effects of a specific form, namely bilinear interactions. It is possible that other, more complex, interaction forms are operative. For example, changes in the slope from regressing drug use onto peer pressure might occur not as a linear function of the quality of the parent-teen relationship but rather as a quadratic function of this variable. In traditional multiple regression analysis, this would be modeled by the following equation:

$$Y = \alpha + \beta_1 X + \beta_2 Z + \beta_3 Z^2 + \beta_4 XZ + \beta_5 XZ^2 + \varepsilon \qquad (4.5)$$

where Y is the criterion measure, X is the predictor of interest, and Z is the moderator variable (see Jaccard, Turrisi, & Wan, 1990, pp. 55-59). It is possible to use the logic developed in this chapter to estimate the regression coefficients in the latent variable version of this model:

$$F_Y = \alpha + \beta_1 F_X + \beta_2 F_Z + \beta_3 F_{z_2} + \beta_4 F_X F_Z + \beta_5 F_X F_{z_2} + \varepsilon \qquad (4.6)$$

For a discussion of this case, see Jöreskog and Yang (1996) and Kenny and Judd (1984).

Product Terms for a Continuous Moderator Variable and a Qualitative Predictor

There are occasions when an investigator is interested in how a continuous moderator variable affects the relationship between a qualitative predictor variable and a continuous criterion. For example, a researcher might study the effects of having a father absent (a single-parent family) versus having a father present (two-parent family) on the intellectual development of young boys. He or she might reason that mean differences in intellectual development as a function of the presence of the father will decrease as the economic status of the mother increases. This line of reasoning cannot be pursued effectively using the multigroup strategy of Chapter 2 because the moderator variable is continuous. Nor can the methods discussed in this chapter be applied easily.

The most effective means of analysis would use a dummy coded variable for father presence and a multiple-indicator representation of economic status and intellectual development (in order to accommodate potential measurement error). The dummy variable would be used to form a product term with the latent predictor, and the analysis would proceed accordingly. Unfortunately, the mathematics underlying the valid execution of such analyses is beyond the scope of this monograph.

Comparison With Traditional Multiple Regression Analysis

The use of product terms between continuous measures using traditional multiple regression analysis is described in Jaccard, Turrisi, and Wan (1990, pp. 20-33). Whereas the strategy in this chapter uses multiple indicators of each variable, traditional regression analysis uses only a single indicator. The presence of multiple indicators permits the estimation of parameters in the context of an error theory, a distinct advantage of the SEM-based approach. The problem of measurement error in traditional analyses with product terms has received considerable attention over the years (see Jaccard, Turrisi, & Wan, 1990, for a summary), and none of the analytic alternatives has been found to be compelling. The SEM-based strategy with multiple indicators has promise, although additional work certainly is needed to further explore the limits of the methodology. Another advantage of the SEM approach is that it can be used in more complex designs that take into account complex error structures underlying the data.

Although the methods described in this chapter have much promise, there are many issues that still need to be explored. The constraints described and the promising results in terms of robustness are predicated on the assumption of multivariate normality in the "main effect" latent variables and the measurement residuals. Without this assumption, the constraints identified are erroneous. Research is needed to explore the robustness of the approach to violations of multivariate normality in the "main effect" latent variables and indicators. We have found in our preliminary work that the model is robust for small to moderate departures from multivariate normality (see Jaccard & Wan, 1995b). There have been no simulations, to our knowledge, on the robustness of maximum likelihood for three-way interactions involving multiple-indicator models.

Alternative Approaches

There have been several approaches proposed that are distinct from the one described here for latent variable product term analysis. The approaches of Ping (1994, 1995) and Jaccard and Wan (1995a) rely on maximum likelihood analysis in LISREL, but they require centering of the raw scores and are not as flexible as the approach described here. The constraints suggested by these authors appear quite different from those described in the present chapter, because centering simplifies many of the mathematical relations between variables and renders negligible the effects of several of the constraints.

Jöreskog and Yang's (1996) approach is superior because it makes use of the relevant means and intercepts in such a way as to provide more sound parameter estimates in the general case of noncentered and centered data. Jaccard and Wan's (1995a) approach used four indicators for the latent product variable and relaxed some of the statistical constraints required of the correlated errors between the product indicators. Their estimation strategy yielded promising results in a simulation study, but we suspect that the Jöreskog and Yang method with a single indicator ultimately will prove to be better. This is because the Jöreskog and Yang method includes intercept terms in the estimation strategy, takes into account mean structures, and minimizes nonnormality in the system by using only a single indicator of the product term.

Research is needed to identify the optimal number of product term indicators for uncovering the population structure given different model constraints. The approach of Ping (1994, 1995, 1996) uses a two-stage estimation strategy that was necessary for

LISREL 7 but is not necessary for LISREL 8. LISREL 8 can accommodate simultaneous estimation of the necessary parameters; hence, the approach described here is preferable to that of Ping. Bollen (in press) has proposed a two-stage least squares analysis of latent variable product terms that appears promising. This approach requires the use of instrumental variables and large sample sizes. It also relies on a limited information (LI) rather than a full information (FI) method of estimating parameters, which can lead to less efficient estimators. The method circumvents the assumption of multivariate normality in the latent variables and has many positive features. Research is needed to explore the relative merits of Bollen's approach and that advocated by Jöreskog and Yang (1996).

The use of product term latent variable modeling is in its infancy, and there is much work that needs to be done before we know its ultimate utility across a range of research conditions. We urge the reader at this point to use these methods with caution and to monitor the statistical literature for advances in this important area of inquiry.

5. GENERAL CONSIDERATIONS

The approaches described in this monograph are useful because they formally take into account measurement error when estimating and testing the statistical significance of interaction effects. This includes both systematic and random error for both cross-sectional and longitudinal designs. The ability to confront the problem of fallible measures is possible because of the presence of multiple indicators for the constructs of interest. This implies that when designing research, investigators should strive to obtain multiple indicators so that measurement error can be accommodated. In this chapter, we discuss practical issues that researchers need to consider when designing studies for SEM-based analyses of interaction effects.

First, we consider alternative methods for obtaining multiple indicators. Second, we discuss decisions concerning sample size and statistical power. Third, we consider methods for testing multivariate normality and potential remedies when nonnormality is present. Fourth, we discuss issues of missing data. Fifth, we discuss the use of fit indices other than the traditional chi-square test of fit. Sixth, we consider issues in the inclusion of covariates and the use of single indicators. Finally, we discuss cautions for SEM analyses of interactions.

Obtaining Multiple Indicators

Multiple indicators are required for the analyses described in this monograph. Sometimes, it is straightforward for investigators to obtain multiple indicators. There may already exist two or three measures that are both practical and psychometrically sound. There are also occasions, however, when an investigator may have only a single measure in which he or she has confidence.

When this is the case, there are several strategies that can be used to generate multiple indicators. If the single measure is a multi-item scale, then one possibility is to create

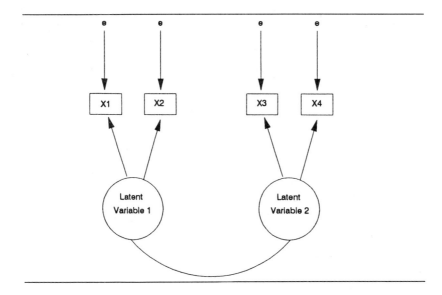

Figure 5.1. Example of Empirical Underidentification

multiple indicators through split-half methods. The items on the scale are randomly divided into two groups of items, then separate scores are calculated for the two "split halves." These two scores then serve as multiple indicators of the same underlying construct. This strategy requires high levels of item homogeneity. A second strategy is to use a test-retest framework. This involves administering the same measure twice, then using the scores at both administrations as multiple indicators of the same construct. This strategy requires that the construct not change between the two administrations and that there are no reactive or memory effects on the second administration as a function of the first administration.

Both the split-half strategy and the test-retest strategy are well known in psychometrics for reliability estimation. The use of them in SEM-based analyses to estimate measurement error and correct for error bias is no more or less prudent than using the strategies to estimate the reliability of a set of measures in the context of traditional psychometric theory. SEM-based approaches go beyond traditional psychometric theory by integrating error theories and conceptual theories and deriving parameter estimates simultaneously in both measurement and structural models.

A second issue concerns how many indicators to have for each construct. Most methodologists recommend at least three. Research strategies with two indicators have the potential for analytic complications resulting from empirical underidentification. This problem is illustrated using the model in Figure 5.1. Consider the left side of this model, in which the focus is on a single latent variable with two indicators. Imagine for the moment that the other latent variable and indicators do not exist. It can be shown mathematically that the correlation between the two indicators must equal the product of the standardized path coefficients from the latent variable to the observed indicators (i.e., $r_{12} = p_{1A}p_{2A}$). There exist an infinite number of pairs of path coefficients that will perfectly reproduce r_{12}. For example, if $r_{12} = 0.24$, then p_{1A} could equal 0.8 and p_{2A} could equal 0.3; or p_{1A} could equal 0.6 and p_{2A} could equal 0.4; and so on. There is no way for LISREL to determine a unique set of values for the path coefficients based only on the single observed correlation, r_{12}. In this case, the model is said to be underidentified, and no solution is possible. By contrast, when there are three indicators for a construct, then a unique solution for the path coefficients exists. This is why use of at least three indicators frequently is recommended. Use of four indicators not only yields a unique solution for the path coefficients but also permits the testing of predicted versus observed correlations for purposes of evaluating model fit. Thus, some methodologists recommend the use of four indicators.

Although our own preference is for the use of three indicators or more, the use of two indicators does not condemn the researcher to underidentified models. Consider the model in Figure 5.1. Although there are only two indicators per latent variable, there is a unique solution for the path coefficients, but only if the correlation between the latent variables is nonzero. If the correlation is zero (or, in practice, near zero), then the underidentification problem will prevail. In essence, the presence of correlation between the latent variables adds a third "indicator" to each latent variable (namely, the other latent variable), yielding a unique solution. The use of two indicators, then, is potentially dangerous because it can (but does not necessarily) result in model underidentification. This is not true when three indicators are used.

Another important measurement issue is the choice of the reference indicator that is used to define the metric of the latent variable. As discussed in previous chapters, the conclusions made with respect to a test of interaction can differ depending on the measure chosen to serve as a reference indicator. Tests of interactions should consider the issue of generalizability across measures, especially when the choice of a reference indicator is arbitrary. In general, the reference indicator should be well entrenched in previous research and have a favorable psychometric history. Ideally, the metric of the reference indicator will have intrinsic meaning, or it will have acquired meaning through its extensive use in the literature.

We have stressed throughout this monograph that a strength of multiple-indicator approaches is the ability to estimate parameters in the presence of a theory of measurement error. This should not be taken to imply that SEM-based analyses can serve as a substitute for poor measures. Indicators with suboptimal reliabilities and questionable psychometric histories can lead the analyst astray quickly. We encourage researchers to use high-quality measures as they approach interaction analysis.

Decisions Concerning Sample Size

The issue of choosing an appropriate sample size when planning a study that uses SEM-based approaches is complex. One issue that must be considered is that of statistical power, or ensuring that the probability of a Type II error is sufficiently low. Procedures have been proposed for conducting power analyses for multiple-indicator structural models (see Jöreskog & Sorbom, 1993; Kaplan, 1995; Saris & Satorra, 1993). In practice, however, it is difficult to perform power analyses for multiple-indicator models such as those described in this monograph prior to study implementation. Power analyses require that the researcher make reasonably accurate estimates of population values for all parameters in a model, a task that is formidable for complex multiple-indicator models. Two or three poor estimates can undermine the power analysis. The situation is complicated by possible nonnormality in the data that can adversely affect power estimates.

An imperfect strategy that we have found useful when planning an SEM study is to employ traditional power analysis for OLS hierarchical regression, in which an effect size estimate is defined for an interaction term as if it were an additional predictor being added to a "main effect" regression equation (see Cohen, 1988). For example, in a traditional regression analysis, one might wish to calculate the approximate sample size necessary to attain power of 0.80 for the case in which the "main effect" population regression model yields a squared multiple correlation of 0.15 and the "main effect plus interaction" population model yields a squared multiple correlation of 0.20 (such that the interaction term adds 5% additional explained variance). If the interaction term consists of a single variable (such as would be the case in a single product term between continuous variables), the approximate sample size needed to achieve power of 0.80 at $\alpha = 0.05$ is 130. This is a "ballpark" estimate of the necessary sample size to achieve reasonable statistical power.

Another approach to power analysis is bootstrap methodology. We develop the logic of this approach using the drug example for product term analysis in Chapter 4. In this study, the investigator collected data on 800 individuals. We begin by making the assumption that the sample data are representative of the population data and proceed to select a random sample of 800 individuals from these sample data using sampling *with* replacement. This is usually done after transforming the original data (see Bollen & Stine, 1993). By using sampling with replacement, the original sample mimics an infinitely large population from which smaller samples are selected. For this new, "bootstrapped" sample, we analyze the data using the LISREL program from the original analysis (i.e., the product term program developed in Chapter 4).

Of central interest is whether the null hypothesis for the coefficient associated with the product term is rejected. Suppose that it is (i.e., the absolute z value associated with it is greater than 1.96). Next, we repeat this process. A random sample of 800 individuals is selected from the original sample, using sampling with replacement. The data again are analyzed using the original LISREL program, and the significance test for the product term coefficient is applied, again noting whether the null hypothesis was rejected. We continue repeating this "bootstrapping" process a large number of times, say 500, performing 500 separate LISREL analyses. Across the 500 analyses, we calculate the proportion of times that the null hypothesis for the product term coefficient was rejected. This proportion is the estimate of the statistical power for the coefficient.

Bootstrap analyses may not seem feasible from a practical point of view. LISREL 8, however, includes a bootstrapping feature that makes such analyses simple to execute.

The approach should not be pursued for power analysis unless the initial model fit in the sample data is quite good. Even then, the results of the bootstrap should be viewed as somewhat crude estimates of power. An advantage of the approach is that it can accommodate nonnormal data in the context of power estimation. It is best suited for power analysis after the sample data have been collected and is of marginal utility in the planning stages of an investigation, when a researcher is trying to decide what sample size should be pursued. It is possible to use pilot data in conjunction with bootstrap methodology to make sample size decisions, but the pilot data set would have to be of sufficient size to guarantee that the sample data are representative of the population, which is unlikely to be the case for most applications. For further discussion of bootstrap procedures, see Stine (1989) and Bollen and Stine (1993).

In addition to statistical power, one must consider the stability of the input covariance matrix when making decisions about sample sizes. For effective analysis, one must obtain a sample covariance matrix that is reasonably stable and that approximates the pattern of covariances in the population. In general, the larger the sample size, the more likely it is that this will be the case, everything else being equal. In the broader literature on factor analysis and other multivariate procedures, many methodologists recommend a sample size based on the number of variables being analyzed (e.g., Baggaley, 1982; Marasculio & Levin, 1983). For example, one rule of thumb states that a researcher should have at least 10 times as many respondents as observed variables. A careful review of the literature reveals considerable discrepancy in the number-of-respondents-to-variables rules that are suggested, with some recommendations being as low as 5 respondents for each variable and others as high as 100 respondents for each variable. Other methodologists do not invoke such rules relating the number of respondents to the number of variables and simply state that a minimal sample size for factor analytic problems is 100 to 200 (e.g., Comrey, 1978; Loo, 1983). Cattell (1978) offers yet another criterion, based on the number of factors expected to underlie the observed variables. Finally, other researchers simply recommend obtaining the largest sample size that is feasible (e.g., Rummel, 1970).

The stability of a covariance matrix is influenced by many factors, including the sample size, the number of variables in the matrix, the magnitude of the covariances within the matrix, and the patterning of the covariances. This makes it difficult to provide any simple rule of thumb for determining an optimal sample size. Guadagnoli and Velicer (1988) reviewed the literature on sample size considerations in factor analysis and principal components analysis and conducted an extensive Monte Carlo study on sample size effects. Consistent with other Monte Carlo studies, they found no support for rules of thumb based on respondents-to-variables criteria. The most important factors influencing the stability of the sample covariance matrix were the absolute sample size and the magnitudes of the path coefficients from the latent constructs to the observed indicators (referred to as "saturation"). When such standardized path coefficients were low (i.e., near 0.40), sample size was quite important. At moderate to high saturation levels (e.g., standardized path coefficients of 0.60 to 0.80), once a certain sample size was achieved, further improvements in stability were small with increasing N. When saturation was high (standardized path coefficients from latent variables to observed indicators of 0.80), sample sizes as low as 50 performed well, even when the number of variables in the covariance matrix was large.

Although the research of Guadagnoli and Velicer must be explored in more depth for the kinds of models described in this monograph, some tentative recommendations for applied researchers can be offered. First, if one has at least three indicators per latent variable and relatively high levels of saturation are expected, then smaller sample sizes (in the 75-100 range) probably will yield a reasonably stable covariance matrix (although such sample sizes may prove to be undesirable in terms of statistical power). When saturation is expected to be moderate (in the 0.60 range), then sample sizes near 150 often will be adequate for obtaining a reasonably stable sample covariance matrix. If sample sizes must be small in such scenarios (because of practical constraints), then consideration should be given to estimating the population covariance matrix using methods that differ from traditional estimation practices and that are amenable to small sample scenarios (Pruzek & Lepak, 1992). With low levels of saturation (0.40 or less), minimal sample sizes should be closer to 300 (although this can be offset partially with a larger number of indicators for each latent variable).

Our simulation studies with product terms employing the analytic strategy described in Chapter 4 used relatively high levels of saturation (near 0.80) with three indicators per latent variable and obtained good results for sample sizes of 175. The reliability of a measure typically will equal the square of the standardized path coefficient from the underlying latent variable to the observed measure (assuming no correlated measurement error). Thus, measures that have a psychometric history with reliability coefficients greater than 0.65 probably will fall into the "high saturation" scenario.

A third issue when making decisions about sample size concerns the behavior of statistical tests that are based on asymptotic theory. The chi-square test of goodness of fit, for example, yields an index that is approximately chi-square distributed, given sufficiently large sample sizes. When sample sizes are small, the sampling distribution of the statistic does not approximate a chi-square distribution. The critical question is "What is a sufficiently large sample size?" There is no simple answer to this question, as much depends on the model being tested and the patterning of the data. Some methodologists (e.g., Boomsma, 1983) have suggested that the minimum sample size be 100 for the chi-square test to be reasonably well behaved. If fit indices that are not sample size dependent are used (see Appendix A), then smaller sample sizes possibly can be accommodated, given sufficient statistical power, a reasonably stable input covariance matrix, and a traditional hypothesis testing approach to parameter estimation.

For the analysis of qualitative moderator variables that use the multigroup strategy (Chapter 2), social scientists sometimes use small sample sizes in each group (because of practical constraints). At issue is the minimum sample size for effective SEM analysis with multiple indicators. In terms of statistical power, our experience has been that sample sizes of less than 50 per group typically will yield unacceptably low levels of power for detecting group differences in slopes across a wide range of social science applications. This may not be the case when population interaction effect sizes are large (accounting for more than 20% of the explained variance), but this is rarely the situation in studies of complex behaviors.

We conducted a multigroup simulation study for a simple regression model with two latent predictors and a single latent criterion, all with three indicators and where the indicators were highly saturated (standardized path coefficients from the latent variable to the observed indicator of 0.83). We found that for a sample size of 75 per group and a moderately sized interaction effect, the parameter estimates yielded by LISREL had only small positive bias. We observed minimal evidence for inflated Type I errors using the nested chi-square test of fit (using an alpha of 0.05, the actual Type I error rate was 0.065) and also observed acceptable levels of statistical power (see Jaccard & Wan, 1994). These results may not generalize to more complex models, but they do suggest that under certain conditions, relatively small sample sizes can be considered.

Summarizing the above, if one has reasonably reliable measures (i.e., reliabilities greater than 0.65), if the expected interaction effect size is of moderate strength (corresponding to about 5% unique explained true score variance, in traditional regression terms), if the data are approximately multivariate normal, and if one desires statistical power of approximately 0.80, then sample sizes near 150 probably will suffice for the kinds of analyses described in Chapters 3 and 4. For the multiple-group analyses in Chapter 2, minimum sample sizes of approximately 100 per group are preferred, but sample sizes as small as 75 per group can be used in some contexts. These recommendations must be viewed as tentative. Exceptions can be found based on the type of model being investigated and the fit criteria being minimized (e.g., Stone & Sobel, 1990). Nevertheless, the guidelines provide the reader with some appreciation for sample size requirements.

Multivariate Normality

When measures are not multivariately normally distributed, then it is possible for maximum likelihood analysis to produce biased standard errors and an ill-behaved chi-square test of overall model fit. An important task for researchers is to determine whether multivariate nonnormality is present and, if so, to decide what to do about it. PRELIS is a computer program that accompanies LISREL and performs normality diagnostics. For each of the input variables, PRELIS provides a measure of skewness and kurtosis as well as a test of whether the skewness or kurtosis is statistically significantly different from 0. In addition, an overall test of multivariate skewness and multivariate kurtosis is provided in the form of a chi-square statistic that can be used to test whether there is a statistically significant difference from multivariate normality. Measures must be univariately normally distributed in order to be multivariately normally distributed. Univariate normality, however, does not guarantee multivariate normality. Univariate normality is a necessary but not sufficient condition for multivariate normality.

In our experience, the tests of significance provided by PRELIS are not very helpful. The sampling distributions of the skewness and kurtosis test statistics tend to be ill behaved relative to the normal or chi-square distributions when sample sizes are less than 300 to 400. When sample sizes are greater than 300, even minor departures from normality can produce sizable z scores in the significance tests. There is a growing body of literature suggesting that maximum likelihood estimation is reasonably robust to many types of violations of multivariate normality. The issue, then, is not whether nonnormality exists, but rather whether the degree of nonnormality is sufficient to disrupt effective data analysis.

Most Monte Carlo studies on the robustness of maximum likelihood analyses report univariate rather than multivariate indices of nonnormality. It is difficult to abstract formal guidelines for what constitutes problematic nonnormality because empirical investigations have varied widely in the sample sizes used, the complexity of the models evaluated, and the nature of the nonnormality, all of which can affect robustness. These complications have resulted in what appear to be conflicting results. For example, some studies find that skewness has trivial effects on parameter estimation and the estimation of standard errors (e.g., Sharma, Durvasula, & Dillon, 1989), whereas other studies report estimation complications as a function of skewness (Kaplan, 1990). Almost all studies find that the chi-square test and corresponding standard errors are sensitive to kurtosis (e.g., Boomsma, 1983; Chou, Bentler, & Satorra, 1991; Harlow, 1985; Hu, Bentler, & Kano, 1992; Sharma, Durvasula, & Dillon, 1989). Positive kurtosis tends to yield negatively biased standard errors for parameter estimates (thereby increasing the chances of a Type I error), and negative kurtosis tends to yield positively biased standard errors for parameter estimates (thereby increasing the probability of a Type II error). Kaplan (1990) suggests that univariate skewness that is less than an absolute value of 1.0 across all variables indicates data that can probably safely use maximum likelihood estimation, although some might argue that this is overly conservative. West, Finch, and Curran (1995) review a wide range of studies on robustness to nonnormality. Bollen (1989) argues for the importance of examining multivariate indices of nonnormality, but again, effective guidelines for how to use such measures in the context of structural equation modeling are lacking. Research is needed to develop practical recommendations that can assist the applied analyst in this regard.

Given unacceptable levels of nonnormality, there are several possible actions that the investigator can pursue. First, one can perform analyses to identify outliers relative to normality. Outliers are small numbers of observations that are highly discrepant from the general pattern of the data and that undermine isolating basic trends in the data. It is possible that nonnormality in the data is the result of a few outliers that, if eliminated from the data set, would permit effective analysis. If an outlier search is successful and a few individuals are dropped from the analysis, then it is important that the researcher identify defining characteristics of the outlier cases, so that generalizations can be tempered accordingly. For example, a study of sexual behavior in college students might find that outliers are older, married students who are returning to college after many years away from school. Such students might be dropped from the analysis and conclusions applied to a population that explicitly excludes such students. Outlier analysis relevant to structural equation models is discussed in Bollen (1987) and Rasmussen (1988).

A second strategy for dealing with nonnormality is to transform the scores on a variable so that they more closely approximate a normal distribution. This can be pursued if the metric of the measure is arbitrary. For example, suppose a researcher develops a scale that measures math potential and uses a 20-item test, such that higher scores (ranging from 0 to 20) imply greater math potential. Ideally, the distribution of the scores on the test should reflect the true underlying distribution of actual math potential. The researcher realizes, however, that the scale is crude and may not map perfectly onto this distribution. Suppose that the researcher believes that the distribution of true math potential is normal. If the observed scores are not normally distributed, then one might question the metric that has been established. It may be possible to transform the scores so that they better approximate a normal distribution, thus providing a better map onto the true distribution of math potential. In this case, the researcher would be justified in pursuing a transformation.

A large number of transformations is available to the analyst. The effect of a transformation depends on the initial distribution of the raw scores and the scale of the scores. For example, a power transformation that squares each raw score can have a different effect if the raw scores range from –10 to +10 as opposed to 0 to 20. Useful procedures for choosing a transformation are described in Atkinson (1985), Daniel and Wood (1980), and Emerson and Stoto (1983).

In contrast, there are circumstances in which transformations may have conceptual as well as measurement implications. For example, suppose one is studying official reports of salary expressed in units of dollars. In this case, there is probably a (near) 1 to 1 correspondence between the observed scores and the true underlying distribution of income, and the metric is not arbitrary. Any transformation changes what is being modeled. A log transformation, for example, would mean that the researcher is no longer modeling dollars but rather is constructing a model of log dollars. Any generalizations from the data with respect to theory must then be to log dollars and not to dollars, because coefficients have been defined so as to minimize errors of prediction for log dollars, not dollars.

Chapter 4 presented a method of interaction analysis that used product terms. Generally speaking, product indicators will have nonnormal distributions, even if the measures used to form the product term are normally distributed and there is no statistical interaction. It is not appropriate to transform the product indicators in order to eliminate nonnormality (although transformations may be appropriate for the indicators of the "main effect" or component variables, prior to the formation of the product indicators). Such transformations violate the integrity of the underlying distributions and their mathematical relations.

A third method for dealing with nonnormality is to use estimation procedures other than maximum likelihood that are robust to violations of multivariate normality. One of the more popular alternatives is ADF or weighted least squares (WLS). Unfortunately, this approach requires rather large sample sizes and has not fared well with research designs that use smaller sample sizes. For a more extensive discussion of WLS estimation, see Bollen (1989), Bentler (1993), and Hu, Bentler, and Kano (1992). Another possibility is the robust maximum likelihood estimation method proposed by Bentler (1993), which is available in the EQS program (but not in LISREL).

A final method for confronting nonnormality is to use bootstrap methodology for purposes of estimating standard errors. Bootstrap estimation of standard errors and the testing of hypotheses may require special transformations of the sample data. For elaboration of the issues involved, see Bollen and Stine (1993).

Missing Data

Researchers occasionally encounter missing data on selected variables. Statisticians have identified several approaches for dealing with missing data. Consider the case of three variables X, Y, and Z. One approach to missing data is to delete any individual from the analysis who has missing data on any of the variables. This is called listwise deletion. A second approach is to delete the individual with missing data on a variable, but only when estimating the parameters that involve the variables on which data are missing. For example, if an individual were missing data only on the X variable, then the individual would be included when calculating the covariance between Y and Z, but not included when calculating the covariance between X and Z. This strategy is called pairwise deletion of missing data. A third approach is to make an intelligent guess about what the person's score on a variable would have been if the data were not missing, then to substitute this value for the missing data. This strategy is called imputation.

One form of imputation involves substituting the mean score of the variable for missing data. If an individual has missing data on X, then the mean score on X across all individuals in the sample is substituted for the missing value. Another form of imputation is to use information from other variables, for which data are not missing, that permit one to accurately predict the missing data for a given individual. For example, using only individuals for whom there are complete data, one could compute a regression equation for predicting X from a set of other variables. If the multiple correlation is large, then one could use the regression equation to calculate a "predicted" score for any individual who is missing data on X but who has data available on the variables in the predictor set. This predicted score would then be imputed for the missing value. Another variant of the imputation strategy is the "hot deck" strategy, in which a missing value for a given individual is replaced by the score of another individual within the data set who has identical scores to the individual with missing data on all other variables (Ford, 1983). A fourth general strategy is to model the pattern of missing data through the use of dummy variables or multiple-group solutions, then introduce formal statistical controls for missing data in the modeling process (see Allison, 1987; Cohen & Cohen, 1983, for examples).

The choice of a method for dealing with missing data depends on many factors, including (a) the sample size, (b) the frequency with which missing data occur and how missing data are patterned across the variables, (c) the magnitude and patterning of the population covariances, (d) the type of analysis being conducted (i.e, the parameters being estimated and the statistical algorithm being used), (e) the ability to derive accurate imputation strategies, and (f) whether the data are missing randomly or systematically. Consideration of relevant choice criteria is beyond the scope of this book. Readers are referred to Timm (1970), Allison (1987), Bollen (1989, pp. 369-376), Muthén and Jöreskog (1983), Muthén, Kaplan, and Hollis (1987), Lee (1986), and Little and Rubin (1987). Some comments about the different strategies are offered here.

If data are missing completely at random (MCAR) and basic model assumptions are met, then listwise deletion provides no particular estimation difficulties, given a sufficiently large sample size. The primary disadvantage of the method is that the loss of cases can be considerable, potentially undermining statistical power and a stable sample covariance matrix. For example, if there are 15 variables and each variable has 5% of its data missing at random, then less than half of the sample will have complete data. Such a drastic reduction in sample size can result in less efficient estimators.

Pairwise deletion strategies can be more efficient for MCAR data, but such strategies introduce additional complications (Browne, 1983). Pairwise deletion of missing data can (but does not necessarily) yield sample covariance matrices that are not positive definite, thereby introducing analytic complications. For example, using pairwise deletion strategies, it is possible to obtain patterns of correlations and covariances that are theoretically impossible. Consider the case of the three possible correlations between the variables X, Y, and Z. Once two of the correlations are known, the third correlation must fall within a certain range. The correlation r_{XY} cannot exceed $r_{XZ} \times r_{YZ} + [(1 - r_{XZ}^2)(1 - r_{YZ}^2)]^{1/2}$ and cannot be less than $r_{XZ} \times r_{YZ} - [(1 - r_{XZ}^2)(1 - r_{YZ}^2)]^{1/2}$. If $r_{XZ} = 0.80$ and $r_{YZ} = 0.40$, then r_{XY} must be between $-.23$ and 0.870. Anything outside this range is impossible. With pairwise deletion of missing data, it is possible for r_{XY} to occur outside this range.

LISREL usually will indicate the presence of such a condition by informing the user that the input matrix is not positive definite (although other conditions can lead to a nonpositive definite input matrix; see Wothke, 1993). When this occurs, the traditional pairwise strategy is problematic.

A second issue in the use of pairwise deletion is how to define the number of observations on the DA line of a LISREL program. Traditional practice is to assign the smallest sample size used in the calculation of the different variances and covariances. It is unclear if this is, indeed, an optimal strategy. In general, the use of a smaller sample size value decreases the value of the chi-square test statistic, leading to a lower probability of model rejection, everything else being equal. Smaller sample size values also increase the standard errors of parameter estimates within the model, thereby lowering statistical power for these significance tests, everything else being equal. One strategy is to evaluate a model using a range of sample size values (e.g., the smallest, the largest, and the average). If the conclusions one makes are the same in each instance, then the choice of a sample size value is not critical. If the conclusions change as a function of sample size, then the conclusions must be tempered accordingly.

The use of imputation strategies raises complex issues. In some respects, imputation is a form of data fabrication (because the analyst makes up values for the missing data), and such an enterprise always must be viewed with concern. Effective use of imputation requires a prediction strategy that leads to accurate imputed values. This may not always be possible from the data at hand. Analysts must provide a well-reasoned criterion for what constitutes an acceptable level of accuracy for purposes of doing imputation. There are few guidelines in the statistical literature in this respect. Even if good prediction is possible, Bollen (1989, pp. 371-372) has shown that some forms of imputation introduce error variance heteroscedasticity and nonnormality into model evaluations. If missing data are minimal, then these violations do not necessarily pose difficulties from the perspective of a hypothesis testing framework (i.e., inflated Type I error rates), given reasonably accurate imputations. In general, it is preferable to use variables outside the theoretical system being evaluated for purposes of developing prediction strategies for imputed values. A promising variant of imputation strategies is the EM method advocated by Little and Rubin (1987; see also the computer program AM in BMDP). This approach has been applied to structural equations with some success (Kiiveri, 1987).

The modeling strategies developed by Allison (1987) and others (e.g., Muthén, Kaplan, & Hollis, 1987) are conceptually elegant but of somewhat restricted practical value for most analytic situations in the social sciences. They require limited and simplistic patterns of missing data that probably occur only rarely in actual research. Nevertheless, they are on firm statistical ground and can deal with scenarios in which data are not MCAR.

Roth (1994) has reviewed the literature on strategies for dealing with missing data. In general, there appears to be little difference in the conclusions one reaches about the statistical significance of parameters when less than 10% of the data are missing completely at random (Gilley & Leone, 1991; Malhotra, 1987; Raymond & Roberts, 1987). In the case of product term analysis (Chapter 4), listwise deletion of missing data generally should be used with respect to the X and Z variables that are used to form the product term, or imputation of the X and/or Z scores should be pursued *prior to* the formation of the product term.

Indices of Fit

Throughout this monograph, we have relied on the traditional chi-square goodness of fit to test interaction effects. We strongly urge the reader to examine additional fit indices beyond the traditional chi-square test when evaluating model fit. The interaction analyses in Chapters 2 and 3 involve nested chi-square difference tests. Such tests of differences in model fit also can be performed for other fit indices. For example, a step 1 program with no constraints on parameter estimation might yield a CFI value of 0.98 (see Appendix A for a discussion of the CFI statistic) as compared with a CFI value of 0.82 when a constraint of equal parameter values is imposed. The difference in the two CFIs of 0.16, which is substantial, implies that the constraint is not viable.

Our experience has been that large changes in fit indices such as the GFI, standardized RMR, CI, CFI, DELTA2, and RMSEA rarely occur when constraints for a single interaction effect are imposed, even when the interaction effect is rather large in magnitude. If the number of observed variables is large and the underlying model being fit to the data is complex, a model can achieve relatively good reproduction of the observed covariance matrix in all respects except for the one or two cells in which the interaction effect might have implications. In this case, the ill fit of the constrained model that implies no interaction can be "swamped" by the good fit of other aspects of the model when calculating the overall fit index. For this reason, we also recommend that researchers pay careful attention to fit statistics that focus on specific parameters within the model as well as specific entries within the covariance matrix (e.g., modification indices and residuals; see Appendix A).

Covariates and Single Indicators

It is often the case that covariates are included in a regression equation. Covariates can be either continuous variables or qualitative variables. When the covariate is a continuous variable, an effective strategy for including the covariate is to obtain multiple indicators of the covariate and then include it in the regression equation. For product term analyses (described in Chapter 4), the mean of the covariate in the KA matrix is fixed to be 0. If the covariate is a qualitative variable (such as religion or gender), then it can be incorporated into the analysis if it is a fixed exogenous variable (see Bollen, 1989, pp. 126-127; Cohen & Cohen, 1983; Muthén, 1989, for details).

Although we strongly advocate the use of multiple indicators, there will be occasions when only a single indicator of one of the constructs in a model is available. Models that have both multiple and single indicators can be programmed using the strategy outlined in this monograph. When a single indicator is used for a latent variable, the path from the latent variable to the indicator should be fixed at 1.00 to provide a metric for the latent variable (i.e., the path cannot be estimated in the LX or LY matrix), and the measurement error for the indicator must be fixed at some value (usually 0 or a value representing an a priori specified amount of measurement error; see the TD or TE matrix). For exceptions to this, see Jöreskog and Sorbom (1993).

Some Cautions

Although the methods described in this monograph have potential, much remains to be done on their applicability. We hope the present treatment will stimulate work in this respect. It will not always be the case that a multiple-indicator SEM approach will be superior to traditional OLS analysis of interactions. OLS is likely to be better when the measures have high reliabilities, sample sizes are small, and departures from multivariate normality are substantial. Readers are urged to familiarize themselves with the growing literature on multiple regression and structural equation models in small sample size and/or distributionally adverse situations, so that intelligent decisions can be made as to appropriate analytic strategy.

SEM strategies are widespread but not without their critics. Cogent critiques have been presented by Rogosa (1987, 1993) and Freedman (1987, 1991). We are sympathetic to many of the issues raised by these critics. Ultimately, researchers must define meaningful theoretical questions and then determine if SEM is an appropriate tool for answering such questions in the context of the collected data and the assumptions that must be made in order to apply the technique effectively. We believe that SEM approaches can have applied value in this context.

APPENDIX A: GOODNESS-OF-FIT INDICES

The general approach of structural equation modeling involves evaluating the viability of a theoretical model by testing whether the model is consistent with a set of data. If

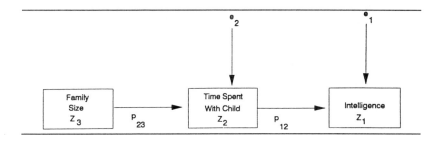

Figure A.1. Path Model of Relationship Between Family Size and Intelligence

the model is consistent with the data, then the model is retained as a viable explanation. If the model is not consistent with the data, then it is rejected.

Consider the model in Figure A.1. This model does not use latent variables and assumes that there is no measurement error in the observed measures (i.e., it is assumed that there is perfect correspondence between the observed measure and the latent variable it represents). Although unrealistic, these simplifications will help us give an intuitive feel for how structural equation modeling operates. The theoretical focus of the model in Figure A.1 is the relationship between the size of the family that a child grows up in and the child's intelligence. According to the model, the size of the family influences the amount of time that a parent can devote to each child. In general, parents with a large number of children devote less time to each individual child than do parents with few children, everything else being equal. This decreased attention from the parent, in turn, negatively affects the intellectual development of the child. In Figure A.1, there are error terms, e_1 and e_2, associated with each Y variable (Z_1 and Z_2). These terms reflect the fact that variables other than those formally specified in the model influence intelligence and the amount of time that parents can give to children. All these other influences are represented in the respective e terms.

We will make some further assumptions in order to simplify presentation, although these are not required in practice. Specifically, we assume that the relationships between variables are linear, that the residuals are uncorrelated with one another, and that the residuals are uncorrelated with the immediate determinants of the Y variable with which the residual is associated.

The model in Figure A.1 can be expressed as a set of linear equations (called structural equations). We state the equations here using standardized scores in order to simplify our presentation further. Although the underlying theory applies only to covariances, the use of standardized variables is pedagogically advantageous. The equations are

$$Z_1 = p_{12}Z_2 + e_1 \tag{A.1}$$

$$Z_2 = p_{23}Z_3 + e_2 \tag{A.2}$$

where Z_1 is the standard score of intelligence, Z_2 is the standard score of time spent with each child, Z_3 is the standard score for family size, and e_1 and e_2 are error terms reflecting factors that influence the criterion variables other than the predictors. (Note: These e should not be confused with the measurement residuals in the LISREL program; in this case, they represent residuals as traditionally represented in multiple regression equations.) The terms p_{12} and p_{23} are called path coefficients. The subscript for a given path coefficient reflects the variable that the path is going to (the first subscript) and the variable that the path is emanating from (the second subscript). It can be seen that the basic form of these equations is the linear model (without the intercept, because we are using standard scores) in which the path coefficients merely reflect standardized regression coefficients. These equations specify the fundamental relationships between variables depicted in Figure A.1. Thus, intelligence is a linear function of time spent with the child, and the time spent with the child is a linear function of family size.

The observed correlation matrix between the three measures is as follows:

	Family Size	Time Spent	IQ
Family Size	1.00	−.30	−.60
Time Spent	−.30	1.00	0.30
IQ	−.60	0.30	1.00

We use a correlation matrix instead of a covariance matrix because all the variables have been standardized. The model in Figure A.1 represents a theory about this correlational structure. According to the model, intelligence and the amount of time that a parent spends with each individual child are correlated *because* the latter variable influences the former variable. Similarly, family size and the amount of time spent with a child are correlated *because* family size influences time spent with the child.

It is possible to express a correlation between any two variables in the system as a function of the path coefficients within the model. Consider, for example, the correlation between intelligence and time spent with the child. A well-known formula for a correlation coefficient is the following:

$$r_{23} = (1/N)\Sigma Z_2 Z_3 \tag{A.3}$$

We now perform some algebraic manipulations on this equation. According to the model in Figure A.1, $Z_2 = p_{23}Z_3 + e_2$. We first substitute the right-hand side of this equation for Z_2 into the formula for r_{23}:

$$r_{23} = (1/N)\Sigma(p_{23}Z_3 + e_2)Z_3 \tag{A.4}$$

We next expand the product of $(p_{23}Z_3 + e_2)Z_3$, so that

$$r_{23} = (1/N)\Sigma(p_{23}Z_3Z_3 + Z_3e_2) \tag{A.5}$$

Next, we break the expression into two separate summations

$$r_{23} = (1/N)\Sigma p_{23}Z_3Z_3 + (1/N)\Sigma Z_3e_2 \qquad (A.6)$$

and because p_{23} is a constant, we bring it to the left of the summation:

$$r_{23} = p_{23}(1/N)\Sigma Z_3Z_3 + (1/N)\Sigma Z_3e_2 \qquad (A.7)$$

Note that the expression $(1/N)\Sigma Z_3Z_3$ is simply the formula for a correlation coefficient. In this case, it is the correlation of Z_3 with itself, which equals 1. Also, the expression $(1/N)\Sigma Z_3e_2$ is a correlation between Z_3 and e_2, which must be zero, given our assumptions. This yields

$$r_{23} = (p_{23})(1.0) + 0$$

$$r_{23} = p_{23} \qquad (A.8)$$

The correlation between Z_2 and Z_3 is simply the path coefficient, p_{23}.

The situation is somewhat more interesting when we examine the correlation between Z_1 and Z_3. Let us repeat the process. The correlation is

$$r_{13} = (1/N)\Sigma Z_1Z_3 \qquad (A.9)$$

According to Figure A.1, $Z_1 = p_{12}Z_2 + e_1$. We therefore substitute the right-hand side of this equation for Z_1 into the formula:

$$r_{13} = (1/N)\Sigma(p_{12}Z_2 + e_1)Z_3 \qquad (A.10)$$

We next expand the product of Z_3 times $(p_{12}Z_2 + e_1)$, so that

$$r_{13} = (1/N)\Sigma(p_{12}Z_2Z_3 + Z_3e_1) \qquad (A.11)$$

Next, we break the expression into two separate summations

$$r_{13} = (1/N)\Sigma p_{12}Z_2Z_3 + (1/N)\Sigma Z_3e_1 \qquad (A.12)$$

and because p_{12} is a constant, we bring it to the left of the summation:

$$r_{13} = p_{12}(1/N)\Sigma Z_2Z_3 + (1/N)\backslash\Sigma Z_3e_1 \qquad (A.13)$$

Note that the expression $(1/N)\Sigma Z_2Z_3$ is the formula for a correlation coefficient and, in this case, it is the correlation of Z_2 and Z_3. As shown above, this correlation equals p_{23}. The expression $(1/N)\Sigma Z_3e_1$ is a correlation between Z_3 and e_1, which is zero. This yields

$$r_{13} = (p_{12})(r_{23}) + 0$$

TABLE A.1
Observed, Predicted, and Residual Matrices

Observed Matrix			Predicted Matrix			Residual Matrix		
1.00	−.30	−.60	1.00	−.30	−.09	0.00	0.00	−.51
−.30	1.00	0.30	−.30	1.00	0.30	0.00	0.00	0.00
−.60	0.30	1.00	−.09	0.30	1.00	−.51	0.00	0.00

$$r_{13} = (p_{12})(p_{23}) \qquad (A.14)$$

In this case, r_{13} equals the product of p_{12} and p_{23}. Because the values of p_{12} and p_{23} are known (they are simply the correlations between the respective variables), we can multiply the two path coefficients from the observed data to obtain a prediction of what the correlation r_{13} should be, if the model in Figure A.1 is correct. The values of p_{12} and p_{23} are 0.30 and −.30, and the product of these two coefficients is −.09. According to the model in Figure A.1, the correlation between family size and IQ should be −.09. The actual correlation between these variables, however, is −.60. The discrepancy between the predicted and observed correlation is large, calling the model into question.

This is a highly simplified example, but it conveys the general logic of SEM analyses. The researcher specifies a conceptual model that he or she believes can account for the variances and covariances among a set of observed measures. Based on this model, LISREL derives a set of path coefficients that reproduce the variances and covariances as well as possible. These predicted variances and covariances are then compared with the observed variances and covariances. If the predicted values are close to the observed values, then the model is said to be consistent with the data. If the predicted values deviate substantially from the model, then the model is rejected.

For the model in Figure A.1, Table A.1 presents the observed correlation matrix, the predicted correlation matrix, and the difference between the two (where each cell of the predicted matrix has been subtracted from the corresponding cell of the observed matrix). This latter matrix is called the residual matrix. A perfect fitting model will yield a residual matrix that has all zeros in it; that is, it will be a zero matrix.

Tautological Predicted and Observed Covariances/Correlations

Inspection of Table A.1 reveals some subtleties in the logic of comparing predicted and observed covariance/correlation matrices in structural equation modeling. On one hand, we are testing the viability of a model by examining how well we can reproduce the correlation matrix between the observed variables using the path coefficients in the model. We also use the correlation matrix to derive the values of the path coefficients. This sometimes leads to cases in which perfect prediction of a correlation is guaranteed because it is a mathematical tautology with the path coefficient(s). For example, we found in our decomposition of correlations that r_{23} equals p_{23}. In this case, the "prediction" of r_{23} from p_{23} is tautological, and perfect "prediction" is guaranteed. This was not true for r_{13}. This correlation, according to the model, should equal $p_{12}p_{23}$, and we found that this was not the case. In short, some of the variances and covariances within the observed covariance matrix will be perfectly reproducible because of mathematical tautologies within the theoretical system, but this will not be true of other variances and covariances. Only in the latter case are comparisons between predicted and observed values meaningful.

There are some models in which every observed variance and covariance will be perfectly predictable because of mathematical tautologies. Such models are said to be *just identified*. These models cannot be evaluated by comparing predicted and observed values. Other models have at least one variance or covariance that is not a mathematical tautology vis-à-vis the underlying path coefficients, and these models are said to be *overidentified*. Overidentified models can be tested meaningfully by comparing predicted and observed values, at least for those relations that are nontautological. There are also situations in which a model is *underidentified*. This occurs when there is no unique solution for the path coefficients and an infinite number of values exists for the path coefficients, all of which result in perfect reproduction of the observed variances and covariances. Such models cannot be tested in structural equation frameworks.

The model in Figure A.1 is an overidentified model because the data provide three observed correlations but there are only two path coefficients to estimate in the model. LISREL performs identification checks for models to ensure that they are not underidentified. One can determine in some cases if a model is just identified or overidentified by examining the degrees of freedom associated with the chi-square test of fit on LISREL output. If a model is just identified, then the chi-square test of goodness of fit will have zero degrees of freedom associated with it. If the model is overidentified, then the chi-square test will have degrees of freedom greater than zero. However, exceptions exist to this rule of thumb.

Deriving Predicted Variances, Covariances, and Correlations

When deriving a set of values for the path coefficients that best reproduce the observed variances and covariances, there are many ways of quantifying the notion of "best." For example, we could calculate path values that minimize the sum of the absolute values of each cell of the residual matrix. Alternatively, we could derive path values that minimize the sum of the square of each element of the residual matrix. Statisticians have found it useful to minimize a maximum likelihood criterion that appears as follows:

$$F_{ML} = \log|S| - \log|\hat{S}| + \text{trace}[(S)(\hat{S}^{-1})] - k \qquad (A.15)$$

where S is the observed sample covariance matrix, $\hat{S}$ is the predicted covariance matrix, k is the order of the sample covariance matrix, and log is the natural log function.[1] Although this fit function appears somewhat formidable, it actually is straightforward. Consider, for example, the case in which there is perfect model fit and S equals $\hat{S}$. In this case, the determinant of S will equal the determinant of $\hat{S}$, and the difference between the logs of these determinants will equal zero. Similarly, $(S)(\hat{S}^{-1})$ will equal an identity matrix with all ones in the diagonal. When the diagonal elements are summed (via the trace function), the result will be the value of k. Subtracting k from this value yields zero. Thus, when there is perfect model fit, F_{ML} equals zero. As model fit becomes worse, values of F_{ML} become larger, everything else being equal.

The reason statisticians prefer to minimize F_{ML} rather than some other criterion is that F_{ML} has useful statistical properties. Specifically, it is possible to calculate estimated standard errors for each path coefficient and to perform traditional tests of statistical significance for the path coefficients using these standard errors. In addition, F_{ML} can be used to define a variety of goodness-of-fit indices for evaluating overall model fit. These will be discussed shortly.

Although F_{ML} has useful statistical properties, there are occasions for which it is ill behaved (see Chapter 1). In these instances, different minimization criteria are used. Alternative fit criteria include unweighted least squares and weighted least squares criteria. Unweighted least squares analysis minimizes the sum of the squared residuals in the residual matrix. Weighted least squares analysis also minimizes the sum of the squared residuals in the residual matrix, but it gives an empirically determined weight to each squared residual before summing them. Thus, some squared residuals are given more weight than others when deriving path coefficients that "best" reproduce the covariance matrix.

Indices of Model Fit

There are many different ways of characterizing the overall degree of correspondence between the predicted and observed covariance matrices in a structural equation analysis. More than 30 such indices have been proposed in the literature, and there is little agreement as to which index is best. In this section, we discuss fit indices that we believe, as a collective, provide useful perspectives on model fit. The choice of indices was based on either tradition or formal reviews of Monte Carlo studies on the fit indices (e.g., Bentler, 1990; Browne & Cudek, 1993; Gerbing & Anderson, 1993).

The traditional measure of model fit is the chi-square fit index. This is simply F_{ML} times $N - 1$, where N is the sample size. When F_{ML} is zero, the chi-square will be zero and perfect model fit will exist. As F_{ML} increases, so does the chi-square statistic, everything else being equal. The chi-square statistic is useful because it provides a formal statistical test of the null hypothesis that there is perfect model fit in the population (i.e., that the residual matrix is all zeros in the population). Statisticians have shown that, under the assumptions discussed in Chapter 1 and with large sample sizes, the product of F_{ML} and $N - 1$ is chi-square distributed with degrees of freedom

$$df = [(.5)(k)(k + 1) + k] - t \qquad (A.16)$$

where k is the order of the input covariance matrix and t is the number of parameters estimated in the model.[2] If the chi-square is statistically significant (e.g., $p < 0.05$), then perfect model fit does not exist in the population. If the chi-square is statistically nonsignificant, this is consistent with perfect model fit.

The chi-square test statistic has been criticized on several grounds. These include the fact that (a) it is not always chi-square distributed for purposes of testing statistical significance, especially for small sample sizes and nonnormal data, and (b) it is influenced by the sample size, such that model evaluations with extremely large sample sizes will almost always lead to model rejection. For these reasons, other fit indices should be examined in addition to the chi-square test.

In general, there are three classes of fit indices. One class measures absolute model fit by comparing, in various ways, predicted versus observed variances and covariances. A second class uses absolute fit indices but includes a penalty function for lack of parsimony. One can always improve model fit by including additional paths (i.e., parameters to estimate) in the model, to the point at which perfect fit is guaranteed (i.e., the model becomes just identified). The second class of fit indices penalizes the researcher for being too liberal in the specification of parameters to be estimated. The third class of fit indices compares the absolute fit of the model to a competing or alternative model that is either a priori specified or imposed arbitrarily on the data. The current wisdom is that evaluation of model fit should use fit indices from all three classes. If good model fit is suggested across diverse indices, then one has increased confidence in the model. If the different fit indices provide different conclusions about the viability of a model, then caution is warranted.

We recommend the following statistics for evaluating model fit. In the first class of absolute fit indices, we recommend the chi-square test, the goodness-of-fit index (GFI), the standardized root mean square residual (standardized RMR), and the centrality index. The goodness-of-fit index is defined as

$$GFI = 1 - (F_{ML}/F_0) \qquad (A.17)$$

where F_0 is the fit function when all parameters in the model are zero (see Jöreskog & Sorbom, 1993, for details). The GFI ranges from 0 to 1.00. The higher the value, the better the model fit. A rule of thumb that has been suggested frequently is that models that yield a GFI lower than 0.90 are of questionable fit. Our recommendation to report this statistic is based more on tradition than on the performance of the statistic in recent Monte Carlo studies.

The standardized RMR index is an average discrepancy between predicted and observed correlations.[3] Thus, a standardized RMR value of 0.10 means that, on average, the predicted and observed correlations deviated by 0.10 correlation units. The smaller the value of the standardized RMR, the better the model fit, with the smallest possible value being zero.

Based on an extensive review of the literature, Gerbing and Anderson (1993) recommend McDonald's (1989) centrality index (CI). CI is not provided by LISREL but can be computed from its output using this formula:

$$CI = \exp(-1/2 \ d) \qquad (A.18)$$

where $d = (\chi^2_M - df_M)/N$ and χ^2_M is the chi-square fit statistic for the model being evaluated, df_M is the degrees of freedom for the model being evaluated, and N is the sample size. CI generally ranges from 0 to 1.00, with higher scores implying better model fit. CI values less than 0.90 suggest a suspect model.

In the second class of fit indices, we recommend the root mean square error of approximation (RMSEA) and the test of close fit statistic associated with it (Steiger & Lind, 1980). The RMSEA is defined as

$$\text{RMSEA} = (\hat{F}_{ML}/df)^{1/2} \qquad (A.19)$$

where df is defined in Equation A.16 and $\hat{F}_{ML}$ is $\{F_{ML} - [df/(N - 1)]\}$ or zero, whichever is larger. The smaller the value of RMSEA, the better the model fit. When fit is perfect, RMSEA will equal zero. Browne and Cudek (1993) suggest that, as a rule of thumb, RMSEA values less than 0.08 imply adequate model fit and values less than 0.05 imply good model fit. Browne and Cudek (1993) also argue that the traditional chi-square test of model fit is too stringent because it tests for perfect model fit in the population. It is rare that a model will yield a perfect population fit; consequently, they have devised an inferential test for a "close"-fitting model, where close is defined as an RMSEA value of 0.05 or less. Thus, the RMSEA statistic often is accompanied by a p value to test for close fit (CFit). If the p value for CFit is nonsignificant (> 0.05), then good model fit is implied.

In the third class of fit indices, we recommend the comparative fit index (CFI), or its nonbounded counterpart, the RNI (Goffin, 1993), which is defined as

$$\text{CFI} = 1 - \tau/\tau_i \qquad (A.20)$$

where τ is $[(N - 1)(F_{ML}) - df]$ or zero, whichever is larger, τ_i is $[(N - 1)(F_{ID}) - df]$ or zero, whichever is larger, and F_{ID} is the value of the maximum likelihood fit function for the "independence" or "null" model. The "null model" is one that posits no correlation between any of the observed variables. Such a model is not viable in most research situations, but it has been used as the standard for defining the CFI. Despite the questionable applicability of the null model, the CFI index has been found to be a well-behaved index of model fit, especially in small sample situations (see Bentler, 1990). The CFI ranges from 0 to 1.0, with larger values implying good model fit. A rule of thumb often suggested is that models with a CFI less than 0.90 are suspect. Gerbing and Anderson (1993) also recommend a fit index suggested by Bollen (1989) called DELTA2. This index is provided in LISREL8, but it is called the Incremental Fit Index (IFI). The larger the value of DELTA2, the better the model fit. DELTA2 will typically range from 0 to 1.0, but it can exceed 1.0.

In sum, a model that yields a statistically nonsignificant chi-square, a small standardized RMR value (less than 0.05), a large GFI (greater than 0.90), a large CI (greater than 0.90), a small RMSEA value (less than 0.08), a nonsignificant test of close fit (CFit), a large CFI value (greater than 0.90), and a large DELTA2 value (greater than 0.90) is probably a model that fits reasonably well. Models that yield uniformly unacceptable values across the fit indices are suspect. When the fit indices do not converge (i.e., some imply good model fit and others imply marginal or poor model fit), then care must be taken in asserting the model. Of the various fit indices, probably the least diagnostic one is the traditional chi-square test, because of the strong statistical assumptions that underlie it. Readers interested in more discussions of the indices are referred to Bollen and Long (1993). For a caution about existing rule-of-thumb guidelines for declaring good model fit, see Hu and Bentler (1995).

In addition to overall model fit indices, LISREL also provides feedback on the fit of a model that is focused on specific features of the model. One such statistic is called a modification index. A modification index is provided for path coefficients or covariances that have been fixed at some a priori value, usually zero. The modification index is an estimate of how much the overall chi-square test of model fit will decrease if the parameter in question is not fixed at zero, but rather is estimated without constraint. A well-fitting model not only will yield satisfactory overall fit indices but also will tend to have modification indices that are small in magnitude.[4] A modification index of approximately 4.0 signifies that a statistically significant ($p < 0.05$) decrease in the chi-square probably will occur if the parameter is freed and the model is re-estimated. A statistically significant decrease in the chi-square, however, does not always translate into an appreciable change in the magnitude of the parameter from the constrained value, and such effect size criteria also should be brought to bear. For a discussion of modification indices, see Kaplan (1990) and the commentaries that follow.

A second specific index of ill fit is the *standardized residual*. A standardized residual is the difference between a specific covariance in the input data matrix and its predicted covariance divided by the estimated standard error of the difference.[5] It is analogous to a standard score in a sampling distribution and can be interpreted roughly as a z score. Large positive or negative values of the standardized residual suggest that the model is producing ill fit with respect to the covariance in question. This ill fit usually can be traced back to a specific portion of the underlying model. In general, a well-fitting model will yield consistently small standardized residuals. The magnitude of a standardized residual is influenced by sample size (with larger sample sizes tending to produce larger standardized residuals, everything else being equal), and this must also be factored into the interpretation of the standardized residual (see Jöreskog & Sorbom, 1993, for a more detailed discussion of this statistic).

A third approach to identifying ill fit at the level of specific parameters is to examine the values of the parameters yielded by LISREL (and their standard errors). If the parameters take on values that do not make statistical sense (e.g., correlations greater than 1.0 or negative variances) or substantive sense, then the model must be questioned accordingly. For a discussion of how to deal with such "offending estimates," see Wothke (1993). For discussion of methods for model evaluation in general, see Jöreskog (1993).

Notes

1. The maximum likelihood minimization function will falter if either S or $\hat{S}$ is not positive definite, that is, nonsingular. With nonpositive definite matrices, it is possible for the log of zero to occur, which is undefined.

2. The degrees of freedom are slightly different for fixed exogenous variables (see Bollen, 1989, p. 127).

3. Technically, it is a root mean square average rather than a simple arithmetic average.

4. There are exceptions to this rule of thumb. See Kaplan (1990).

5. This LISREL-based definition of a standardized residual is not the same in different SEM computer packages. For example, the EQS computer program defines a standardized residual in terms of the difference between the predicted and observed correlation coefficient.

APPENDIX B: DATA SETS USED IN EXAMPLES

This appendix presents the covariance matrices for all the analyses reported in this monograph. Data are in lower triangular form. The variables are in the same order as on the LA line described in the program in the corresponding chapter. If a data set is omitted, then it already has been given in the text.

Chapter 2

Gender as a Moderator of the Relationship Between Perceived Personableness and Success

MALES							FEMALES						
21.1							39.4						
18.5	21.4						37.1	39.2					
19.3	19.2	21.1					37.9	37.6	40.5				
5.3	5.6	5.7	7.9				11.1	11.2	11.4	7.8			
5.0	4.8	5.2	5.2	6.5			10.0	9.8	10.3	5.2	6.9		
5.1	5.3	5.2	0.2	0.0	6.3		5.3	5.7	5.5	0.2	0.9	6.8	
5.4	5.6	5.3	0.1	0.0	4.7	6.7	5.6	6.1	5.5	0.1	0.0	4.5	6.7

Ethnic Group as a Moderator of the Relationship Between Perceived Personableness and Success

AFRICAN AMERICANS							HISPANICS						
21.3							39.5						
18.1	21.5						37.3	39.3					
19.7	19.1	21.3					38.2	37.3	40.6				
5.3	5.3	5.7	7.5				11.5	11.3	11.6	7.5			
5.0	4.7	5.1	5.4	6.3			10.3	9.6	10.2	5.5	6.7		
5.4	5.3	5.5	0.3	0.1	6.1		5.7	5.5	5.7	0.1	0.7	6.3	
5.0	5.5	5.9	0.2	0.1	4.5	6.5	5.6	6.3	5.9	0.2	0.1	4.9	6.8

WHITES
25.1		
21.9	22.9	
22.5	21.3	24.1

```
3.2   2.3   2.7   8.4
3.9   3.4   3.2   3.7   4.9
8.4   9.0   8.3   2.2   1.2   7.3
8.9   9.5   9.2   1.8   1.3   5.9   8.6
```

Gender and Party Identification (Democrats vs. Republicans) as a Moderator of the Relationship Between Judgments of Personableness and Judgments of Success

MALE DEMOCRATS	FEMALE DEMOCRATS

```
21.0                                21.0                 20.4
18.9 21.0                           18.5 20.6
19.5 19.2 21.7                      19.1 18.9 21.5
 5.6  5.6  5.9  7.6                  4.3  4.3  4.6  8.1
 5.0  4.8  5.2  5.2  6.8            4.9  4.9  5.2  5.5  6.7
 5.2  5.4  5.3  0.2  0.0  6.5       5.7  5.9  5.7  0.6  0.4  6.6
 5.5  5.8  5.5  0.1  0.0  4.8  6.9  5.7  6.2  5.9  0.0  0.0  4.9  7.2
```

MALE REPUBLICANS	FEMALE REPUBLICANS

```
25.1                                39.2
21.9 22.9                           37.1 39.1
22.5 21.3 24.1                      38.0 37.6 40.3
 3.2  2.3  2.7  8.4                 11.1 11.2 11.4  7.6
 3.9  3.4  3.2  3.7  4.9           10.1  9.9 10.3  5.2  6.8
 8.4  9.0  8.3  2.2  1.2  7.3       5.5  5.7  5.5  0.2  0.9  6.5
 8.9  9.5  9.2  1.8  1.3  5.9  8.6  5.8  6.1  5.8  0.1  0.0  4.8  6.9
```

Gender and Party Identification (Democrats vs. Republicans vs. Independents) as a Moderator of the Relationship Between Judgments of Personableness and Judgments of Success

MALE INDEPENDENTS	FEMALE INDEPENDENTS

```
24.2                                25.3
21.5 22.7                           21.5 22.7
22.9 22.1 25.6                      22.3 21.2 24.3
 6.7  6.5  6.9  8.2                  7.4  6.4  6.6  8.5
 5.4  5.3  5.8  5.2  6.1            4.8  4.5  4.3  4.8  4.8
 6.3  6.6  6.5  1.2  0.8  6.6       8.3  9.1  8.4  2.3  1.3  7.4
 6.9  7.2  7.3  0.6  0.8  5.2  7.8  8.8  9.4  9.3  1.9  1.4  5.8  8.8
```

Note: Use the same data from the previous example with the following two groups added).

Chapter 3

Age (7-year-olds vs. 12-year-olds vs. 17-year-olds) as a Moderator
of the Relationship Between Maternal Warmth and Social Development

```
80.5
58.6 56.5
53.5 44.3 49.9
11.4 10.2 10.0  5.9
10.8  8.9  8.9  3.6  4.2
11.3  9.0  8.9  3.7  3.1  4.4
18.9 14.9 14.6  3.4  5.9  4.1 59.6
15.5 12.9 13.5  2.3  4.8  3.6 41.8 45.4
13.7 11.7 12.4  2.4  4.5  3.0 41.7 37.4 47.3
 9.9  7.4  7.1  2.4  2.2  2.3  7.9  6.6  5.6  5.5
 8.1  6.5  5.9  2.2  2.1  2.2  7.1  6.3  5.6  3.4  4.3
 6.3  5.3  4.7  1.7  1.8  1.6  5.8  5.0  4.4  3.2  2.6  3.5
17.6 14.8 14.6  2.7  2.8  3.1 12.1  9.5 11.7  2.2  2.7  1.2 51.7
18.5 16.6 15.2  3.0  2.5  3.0  7.5  4.5  8.1  1.7  2.6  1.7 38.1 45.3
14.7 14.1 11.7  3.0  2.7  3.0  8.8  6.4  9.8  2.8  2.3  1.7 36.3 32.7 41.2
 7.5  6.7  5.6  2.3  2.0  2.2  4.3  4.6  4.2  2.1  2.4  1.7  5.6  6.1  6.1  5.3
 7.2  5.9  5.2  2.1  1.9  1.9  2.3  2.1  2.0  1.5  1.9  1.2  4.0  4.9  4.2  3.1  3.9
 9.0  7.2  5.4  2.0  1.8  1.8  3.7  3.6  2.9  2.1  2.2  1.5  5.2  5.7 5.0  3.6  3.0  4.7
```

Gender and Age as Moderators of the Relationship
Between Maternal Warmth and Social Development

MALES

```
85.3
63.8 62.1
59.6 47.7 54.1
13.7 11.2 10.9  5.8
11.5  9.4  8.9  3.6  4.1
12.6 10.3  9.9  3.6  3.0  4.7
19.0 14.0 14.7  3.3  4.9  3.2 52.9
13.6 10.7 14.5  1.5  3.2  2.4 35.4 43.1
16.1 13.0 14.7  2.1  3.8  2.1 33.1 30.5 39.7
11.1  8.1  8.7  2.5  2.0  2.5  3.6  2.7  1.4  5.3
 8.9  7.3  7.2  2.3  2.1  2.1  4.7  3.1  2.8  3.3  4.0
 7.1  5.9  6.1  1.8  1.7  1.6  3.5  2.4  2.0  3.0  2.6  3.4
```

FEMALES

```
84.7
62.8 60.8
59.3 47.0 53.6
31.7 24.5 25.2 75.4
23.7 19.3 22.7 53.9 58.2
26.4 21.6 23.0 50.3 44.7 52.5
13.6 11.0 10.8  6.8  4.3  4.9  5.7
11.3  9.2  8.8  7.9  5.7  6.2  3.5  4.0
12.3 10.1  9.8  6.1  4.9  4.5  3.5  3.0  4.6
10.8  7.8  8.4  9.2  7.5  6.2  2.4  2.0  2.3  5.2
 8.8  7.2  7.1  9.4  7.0  6.7  2.2  2.1  2.1  3.2  3.9
 6.9  5.8  5.9  7.7  5.9  5.5  1.8  1.7  1.5  3.0  2.5  3.4
```

Chapter 4

Quality of the Parent-Teen Relationship as a Moderator of the Relationship Between Peer Pressure and Drug Use

COVARIANCE MATRIX

```
 2.05
 1.56  1.60
 1.54  1.33  1.59
 0.42  0.34  0.36  0.58
 0.28  0.22  0.25  0.29  0.26
 0.25  0.22  0.22  0.30  0.19  0.28
-0.05 -0.03 -0.05  0.26  0.15  0.16  0.76
 0.00 -0.01 -0.03  0.20  0.11  0.13  0.48  0.42
-0.03 -0.01 -0.04  0.19  0.11  0.12  0.47  0.33  0.42
-0.38 -0.36 -0.33  0.02 -0.01  0.00  0.04  0.03  0.02  0.51
```

Means
```
 3.74  3.68  3.69  0.01  3.01  2.99  0.01  0.00 -0.01  0.26
```

REFERENCES

AIKEN, L., and WEST, S. (1991) *Multiple Regression*. Newbury Park, CA: Sage.

ALEXANDER, R. A., and DeSHON, R. P. (1994) "Effect of error variance heterogeneity on the power of tests for regression slope differences." *Psychological Bulletin* 115: 308-313.

ALLISON, P. (1987) "Estimation of linear models with incomplete data." In C. C. Clogg (Ed.), *Sociological Methodology* (pp. 71-103). San Francisco: Jossey-Bass.

ANDERSON, N. H. (1981) *Foundations of Information Integration Theory*. New York: Academic Press.

ANDERSON, N. H. (1982) *Methods of Information Integration Theory*. New York: Academic Press.

ANDERSON, T. W. (1984) *An Introduction to Multivariate Statistical Analysis*. New York: Wiley.

ATKINSON, A. C. (1985) *Plots, Transformations and Regression*. Oxford, UK: Clarendon.

BAGGALEY, A. R. (1982) "Deciding on the ratio of the number of subjects to number of variables in factor analysis." *Multivariate Experimental Clinical Research* 6: 81-85.

BENTLER, P. (1990) "Comparative fit indices in structural models." *Psychological Bulletin* 107: 238-246.

BENTLER, P. M. (1993) *EQS Program Manual*. Los Angeles: BMD.

BERRY, W. D. (1993) *Understanding Regression Assumptions*. Sage University Papers series on Quantitative Applications in the Social Sciences, 07-092. Newbury Park, CA: Sage.

BIELBY, W. T. (1986a) "Arbitrary metrics in multiple indicator models." *Sociological Methods and Research* 15: 3-23.

BIELBY, W. T. (1986b) "Arbitrary normalizations." *Sociological Methods and Research* 15: 62-63.

BOHRNSTEDT, G. W., and CARTER, T. M. (1971) "Robustness in regression analysis." In H. L. Costner (Ed.), *Sociological Methodology* (pp. 118-146). San Francisco: Jossey-Bass.

BOLLEN, K. A. (1987) "Outliers and improper solutions: A confirmatory factor analysis example." *Sociological Methods and Research* 15: 375-384.

BOLLEN, K. A. (1989) *Structural Equations With Latent Variables*. New York: Wiley.

BOLLEN, K. A. (in press) "Structural equation models that are non-linear in latent variables: A least squares estimator." *Sociological Methodology*.

BOLLEN, K. A., and LONG, J. S. (Eds.) (1993) *Testing Structural Equation Models*. Newbury Park, CA: Sage.

BOLLEN, K. A., and STINE, R. A. (1993) "Bootstrapping goodness of fit measures in structural equation models." In K. A. Bollen and J. S. Long (Eds.), *Testing Structural Equation Models* (pp. 111-135). Newbury Park, CA: Sage.

BOOMSMA, A. (1983) *On the Robustness of LISREL (Maximum Likelihood Estimation) Against Small Sample Size and Non-normality*. Unpublished doctoral dissertation, University of Groningen, The Netherlands.

BRAY, J. H., and MAXWELL, S. E. (1985) *Multivariate Analysis of Variance*. Sage University Papers series on Quantitative Applications in the Social Sciences, 07-054. Beverly Hills, CA: Sage.

BROWNE, M. W. (1983) "Asymptotic comparison of missing data procedures for estimating factor loadings." *Psychometrika* 48: 269-291.

BROWNE, M. W., and CUDEK, R. (1993) "Alternative ways of assessing model fit." In K. Bollen and J. S. Long (Eds.), *Testing Structural Equation Models* (pp. 136-162). Newbury Park, CA: Sage.

BUSEMEYER, J., and JONES, L. (1983) "Analysis of multiplicative combination rules when the causal variables are measured with error." *Psychological Bulletin* 93: 549-562.

95

BYRNE, B. M., SHAVELSON, R. J., and MUTHÉN, B. (1989) "Testing for the equivalence of factor covariance and mean structures: The issue of partial measurement invariance." *Psychological Bulletin* 105: 456-466.

CATTELL, R. B. (1978) *The Scientific Use of Factor Analysis in Behavioral and Life Sciences.* New York: Plenum.

CHOU, C. P., BENTLER, P., and SATORRA, A. (1991) "Scaled test statistics and robust standard errors for non-normal data in covariance structure analysis: A Monte Carlo study." *British Journal of Mathematical and Statistical Psychology* 44: 347-357.

COHEN, J. (1988) *Statistical Power Analysis for the Behavioral Sciences.* Hillsdale, NJ: Lawrence Erlbaum.

COHEN, J., and COHEN, P. (1983) *Applied Multiple Regression/Correlation for the Behavioral Sciences.* Hillsdale, NJ: Lawrence Erlbaum.

COLE, D. A., MAXWELL, S. E., ARVEY, R., and SALAS, E. (1993) "Multivariate group comparisons of variable systems: MANOVA and structural equation modeling." *Psychological Bulletin* 114: 174-184.

COMREY, A. L. (1978) "Common methodological problems in factor analytic studies." *Journal of Consulting and Clinical Psychology* 46: 648-659.

CUDEK, R. (1989) "Analysis of correlation matrices using covariance structure models." *Psychological Bulletin* 105: 317-326.

DANIEL, C., and WOOD, F. S. (1980). *Fitting Equations to Data.* New York: Wiley.

EMERSON, J. D., and STOTO, M. A. (1983) "Transforming data." In D. C. Hoaglin, F. Mosteller, and J. Tukey (Eds.), *Understanding Robust and Exploratory Data Analysis* (pp. 97-127). New York: Wiley.

FORD, B. L. (1983) "An overview of hot-deck procedures." In W. G. Madow, I. Olkin, and D. B. Rubin (Eds.), *Incomplete Data in Sample Surveys* (Vol. 2, pp. 185-207). New York: Academic Press.

FREEDMAN, D. A. (1987) "As others see us: A case study in path analysis." *Journal of Educational Statistics* 12: 101-128.

FREEDMAN, D. A. (1991) "Statistical methods and shoe leather." In P. Marsden (Ed.), *Sociological Methodology 1991* (pp. 222-242). Washington, DC: American Sociological Association.

GERBING, D. W., and ANDERSON, J. C. (1993) "Monte Carlo evaluations of goodness of fit indices for structural equation models." In K. Bollen and J. S. Long (Eds.), *Testing Structural Equation Models* (pp. 40-65). Newbury Park, CA: Sage.

GILLEY, O. W., and LEONE, R. P. (1991) "A two stage imputation procedure for item nonresponse in surveys." *Journal of Business Research* 22: 281-291.

GOFFIN, R. D. (1993) "A comparison of two new indices for the assessment of fit in structural equation models." *Multivariate Behavioral Research* 28: 205-214.

GUADAGNOLI, E., and VELICER, W. F. (1988) "Relation of sample size to the stability of component patterns." *Psychological Bulletin* 103: 265-275.

HARLOW, L. L. (1985) *Behavior of Some Elliptical Theory Estimators With Non-Normal Data in a Covariance Structure Framework: A Monte Carlo Study.* Unpublished doctoral dissertation, University of California, Los Angeles.

HENRY, N. W. (1986) "On arbitrary metrics and normalization issues." *Sociological Methods and Research* 15: 59-61.

HOLLAND, B. S., and COPENHAVER, M. (1988) "Improved Bonferroni-type multiple testing procedures." *Psychological Bulletin* 104: 145-149.

HOLM, S. (1979) "A simple sequentially rejective multiple test procedure." *Scandinavian Journal of Statistics* 6: 65-70.

HU, L., and BENTLER, P. M. (1995) "Evaluating model fit." In R. H. Hoyle (Ed.), *Structural Equation Modeling: Concepts, Issues, and Applications* (pp. 76-99). Thousand Oaks, CA: Sage.

HU, L., BENTLER, P. M., and KANO, Y. (1992) "Can test statistics in covariance structure analysis be trusted?" *Psychological Bulletin* 112: 351-362.

JACCARD, J., BECKER, M., and WOOD, G. (1984) "Pairwise multiple comparisons: A review." *Psychological Bulletin* 96: 589-596.

JACCARD, J., TURRISI, R., and WAN, C. K. (1990) *Interaction Effects in Multiple Regression.* Sage University Papers series on Quantitative Applications in the Social Sciences, 07-072. Newbury Park, CA: Sage.

JACCARD, J., and WAN, C. K. (1994) *Measurement Error in the Analysis of Interaction Effects With Qualitative Moderator Variables and Continuous Predictor Variables: A Multiple Indicator Approach.* Unpublished manuscript, University at Albany, State University of New York.

JACCARD, J., and WAN, C. K. (1995a) "Measurement error in the analysis of interaction effects between continuous predictors using multiple regression: Multiple indicator and structural equation approaches." *Psychological Bulletin* 117: 348-357.

JACCARD, J., and WAN, C. K. (1995b) *Non-Normality in Latent Variables in the Estimation of Coefficients Associated With Product Terms.* Unpublished manuscript, University at Albany, State University of New York.

JOHNSTON, J. (1984) *Econometric Methods.* New York: McGraw-Hill.

JÖRESKOG, K. (1993) "Testing structural equation models." In K. Bollen and J. S. Long (Eds.), *Testing Structural Equation Models* (pp. 294-316). Newbury Park, CA: Sage.

JÖRESKOG, K., and SORBOM, D. (1993) *LISREL VIII.* Chicago: Scientific Software.

JÖRESKOG, K., and YANG, F. (1996) "Non-linear structural equation models: The Kenny-Judd model with interaction effects." In G. Marcoulides and R. Schumacker (Eds.), *Advanced Structural Equation Modeling* (pp. 57-88). Hillsdale, NJ: Lawrence Erlbaum.

KAPLAN, D. (1990) "Evaluating and modifying covariance structure models: A review and recommendation." *Multivariate Behavioral Research* 25: 137-155.

KAPLAN, D. (1995) "Statistical power in structural equation modeling." In R. H. Hoyle (Ed.), *Structural Equation Modeling: Concepts, Issues, and Applications* (pp. 100-117). Thousand Oaks, CA: Sage.

KENNY, D. A. (1979) *Correlation and Causation.* New York: Wiley.

KENNY, D. A., and JUDD, C. M. (1984) "Estimating the nonlinear and interactive effects of latent variables." *Psychological Bulletin* 96: 201-210.

KEPPEL, G. (1982) *Design and Analysis: A Researcher's Handbook* (2nd ed.). Englewood Cliffs, NJ: Prentice Hall.

KIIVERI, H. T. (1987) "An incomplete data approach to the analysis of covariance structures." *Psychometrika* 52: 539-554.

KIM, J., and FERREE, G. (1981) "Standardization in causal analysis." *Sociological Methods and Research* 10: 22-43.

KUHNEL, S. (1988) "Testing MANOVA designs with LISREL." *Sociological Methods and Research* 16: 504-523.

LEE, S. Y. (1986) "Estimation for structural equation models with missing data." *Psychometrika* 51: 93-99.

LITTLE, R., and RUBIN, D. (1987) *Statistical Analysis With Missing Data.* New York: Wiley.

LOEHLIN, J. C. (1987) *Latent Variable Models: An Introduction to Factor, Path, and Structural Analysis.* Hillsdale, NJ: Lawrence Erlbaum.

LOO, R. (1983) "Caveat on sample sizes in factor analysis." *Perceptual and Motor Skills* 56: 371-374.

McCLELLAND, G. H., and JUDD, C. M. (1993) "Statistical difficulties of detecting interactions and moderator effects." *Psychological Bulletin* 114: 376-389.

McDONALD, R. (1989) "An index of goodness of fit based on non-centrality." *Journal of Classification* 6: 97-103.

MALHOTRA, N. K. (1987) "Analyzing marketing research data with incomplete information on the dependent variable." *Journal of Marketing Research* 24: 74-84.

MARASCUILO, L. A., and LEVIN, J. R. (1983) *Multivariate Statistics in the Social Sciences.* Monterey, CA: Brooks/Cole.

MUTHÉN, B. (1989) "Latent variable modeling in heterogeneous populations." *Psychometrika* 54: 557-585.

MUTHÉN, B., and JÖRESKOG, K. (1983) "Selectivity problems in quasi-experimental studies." *Evaluation Review* 7: 807-811.

MUTHÉN, B., KAPLAN, D., and HOLLIS, M. (1987) "On structural equation modeling with data that are not missing completely at random." *Psychometrika* 52: 431-462.

PING, R. A. (1994) "Does satisfaction moderate the association between alternative attractiveness and exit intention in a marketing channel?" *Journal of the Academy of Marketing Science* 22: 364-371.

PING, R. A. (1995) "A parsimonious estimating technique for interaction and quadratic latent variables." *Journal of Marketing Research* 42: 336-347.

98

PING, R. A. (1996) "Latent variable interaction and quadratic effect estimation: A two-step technique using structural equation analysis." *Psychological Bulletin, 119,* 166-175.

PRUZEK, R. M., and LEPAK, G. M. (1992) "Weighted structural regression: A broad class of adaptive methods for improving linear prediction." *Multivariate Behavioral Research* 27: 95-129.

RASMUSSEN, J. (1988) "Evaluating outlier identification tests: Mahalanbois D squared and Comrey's Dk." *Multivariate Behavioral Research* 23: 189-202.

RAYMOND, M. R., and ROBERTS, D. M. (1987) "A comparison of methods for treating incomplete data in selection research." *Educational and Psychological Measurement* 9: 395-420.

ROGOSA, D. R. (1987) "Causal models do not support scientific conclusions: A comment in support of Freedman." *Journal of Educational Statistics* 12: 185-195.

ROGOSA, D. R. (1993) "Individual unit models versus structural equations: Growth curve examples." In K. Haagen, D. Bartholomew, and M. Deistler (Eds.), *Statistical Modeling and Latent Variables* (pp. 259-281). New York: North Holland.

ROTH, P. L. (1994) "Missing data: A conceptual review for applied psychologists." *Personnel Psychology* 47: 537-560.

RUMMEL, R. (1970) *Applied Factor Analysis.* Evanston, IL: Northwestern University Press.

SARIS, W. E., and SATORRA, A. (1993) "Power evaluations in structural equation models." In K. Bollen and J. S. Long (Eds.), *Testing Structural Equation Models* (pp. 181-204). Newbury Park, CA: Sage.

SEAMAN, M. A., LEVIN, K. R., and SERLIN, R. C. (1991) "New developments in pairwise multiple comparisons: Some powerful and practicable procedures." *Psychological Bulletin* 110: 577-586.

SHARMA, S., DURVASULA, S., and DILLON, W. (1989) "Some results on the behavior of alternate covariance structure estimation procedures in the presence of non-normal data." *Journal of Marketing Research* 26: 214-221.

SOBEL, M. E., and ARMINGER, G. (1986) "Platonic and operational true scores in covariance structure analysis." *Sociological Methods and Research* 15: 44-58.

STEIGER, J. H., and LIND, J. C. (1980) *Statistically Based Tests for the Number of Common Factors.* Paper presented at the Annual Meeting of the Psychometric Society, Iowa City.

STINE, R. (1989) "Introduction to bootstrap methods: Examples and ideas." *Sociological Methods and Research* 8: 243-291.

STONE, C. A., and SOBEL, M. E. (1990) "The robustness of estimates of total indirect effects in covariance structure models estimated by maximum likelihood." *Psychometrika* 55: 337-352.

STONE, E. F., and HOLLENBECK, J. R. (1989) "Clarifying some controversial issues surrounding statistical procedures for detecting moderator variables: Empirical evidence and related matters." *Journal of Applied Psychology* 74: 3-10.

TIMM, N. (1970) "The estimation of variance-covariance and correlation matrices from incomplete data." *Psychometrika* 35: 417-438.

TOWNSEND, J. T. (1990) "Truth and consequences of ordinal differences in statistical distributions: Toward a theory of hierarchical inference." *Psychological Bulletin* 108: 551-569.

TOWNSEND, J., and ASHBY, F. (1984) "Measurement scales and statistics: The misconception misconceived." *Psychological Bulletin* 96: 394-401.

WEGENER, B. (1982) *Social Attitudes and Psychological Measurement.* Hillsdale, NJ: Lawrence Erlbaum.

WEST, S., FINCH, J. F., and CURRAN, P. J. (1995) "Structural equation models with nonnormal variables: Problems and remedies." In R. H. Hoyle (Ed.), *Structural Equation Modeling: Concepts, Issues, and Applications* (pp. 56-75). Thousand Oaks, CA: Sage.

WILLIAMS, R., and THOMSON, E. (1986a) "Normalization issues in latent variable modeling." *Sociological Methods and Research* 15: 24-43.

WILLIAMS, R., and THOMSON, E. (1986b) "Problems needing solutions or solutions needing problems?" *Sociological Methods and Research* 15: 64-68.

WOTHKE, W. (1993) "Nonpositive definite matrices in structural equation modeling." In K. Bollen and J. S. Long (Eds.), *Testing Structural Equation Models* (pp. 256-293). Newbury Park, CA: Sage.

ABOUT THE AUTHORS

JAMES JACCARD is Professor of Psychology at the University at Albany, State University of New York. He is director of the Center for Applied Psychological Research. His primary research interests are in the areas of the psychology of population dynamics and adolescent risk behavior, with an emphasis on adolescent unintended pregnancy and adolescent drunk driving. His work has focused on family-based approaches to dealing with adolescent problem behaviors.

CHOI K. WAN is Senior Research Scientist in the Center for Applied Psychological Research at the University at Albany, State University of New York. His research interests include health psychology, behavioral medicine, and social support. His quantitative research interests include meta-analysis, time series analysis, and the analysis of interaction effects.